This book belongs to:

_____
- - - - - - - - - - - - - - -
_____

Copyright © S&M Readers Publishing 2020
All Rights Reserved

What are sight words?

Sight words are words that should be memorized to help a child learn to read and write. Learning sight words allows a child to recognize these words at a glance — on sight — without needing to break the words down into their individual letters and is the way strong readers recognize most words. Knowing common, or high frequency, words by sight makes reading easier and faster, because the reader does not need to stop to try and sound out each individual word, letter by letter.

When to Start Teaching Sight Words?

Before a child starts learning sight words, it is important that he/she be able to recognize and name all the lower-case letters of the alphabet. When prompted with a letter, the child should be able to name the letter quickly and confidently. Note that, different from learning phonics, the child does not need to know the letters' sounds.

Index

SIGHT WORD	PAGE	SIGHT WORD	PAGE
a	8	play	32
and	9	red	33
big	10	run	34
away	11	said	35
can	12	see	36
come	13	the	37
down	14	three	38
find	15	to	39
for	16	two	40
funny	17	up	41
go	18	where	42
help	19	yellow	43
here	20	you	44
in	21	all	45
jump	22	am	46
is	23	are	47
little	24	at	48
it	25	ate	49
look	26	be	50
me	27	black	51
make	28	but	52
my	29	brown	53
not	30	did	54
one	31	came	55

do	56	this	82
eat	57	want	83
four	58	too	84
get	59	well	85
good	60	was	86
he	61	went	87
have	62	what	88
into	63	white	89
like	64	who	90
must	65	will	91
new	66	yes	92
no	67	with	93
our	68	after	94
please	69	an	95
out	70	again	96
pretty	71	any	97
ran	72	as	98
ride	73	ask	99
say	74	by	100
so	75	could	101
she	76	fly	102
soon	77	from	103
that	78	going	104
there	79	had	105
they	80	has	106
under	81	how	107

a

Sight word n°1: a

Use "a" before words that start with a consonant sound and "an" before words that start with a vowel sound.

Say the word out loud and then write it:

a   a   a   a   a   a

Write the word:

Read the following sentence and circle the word:

This is a huge elephant!

Write in the missing word:

This is __ huge elephant!

Color the animal that has the word "a":

a   go   The

Sight word n°2: and

The word and is a conjunction, and when a conjunction joins two independent clauses, you should use a comma with it. The proper place for the comma is before the conjunction.

and

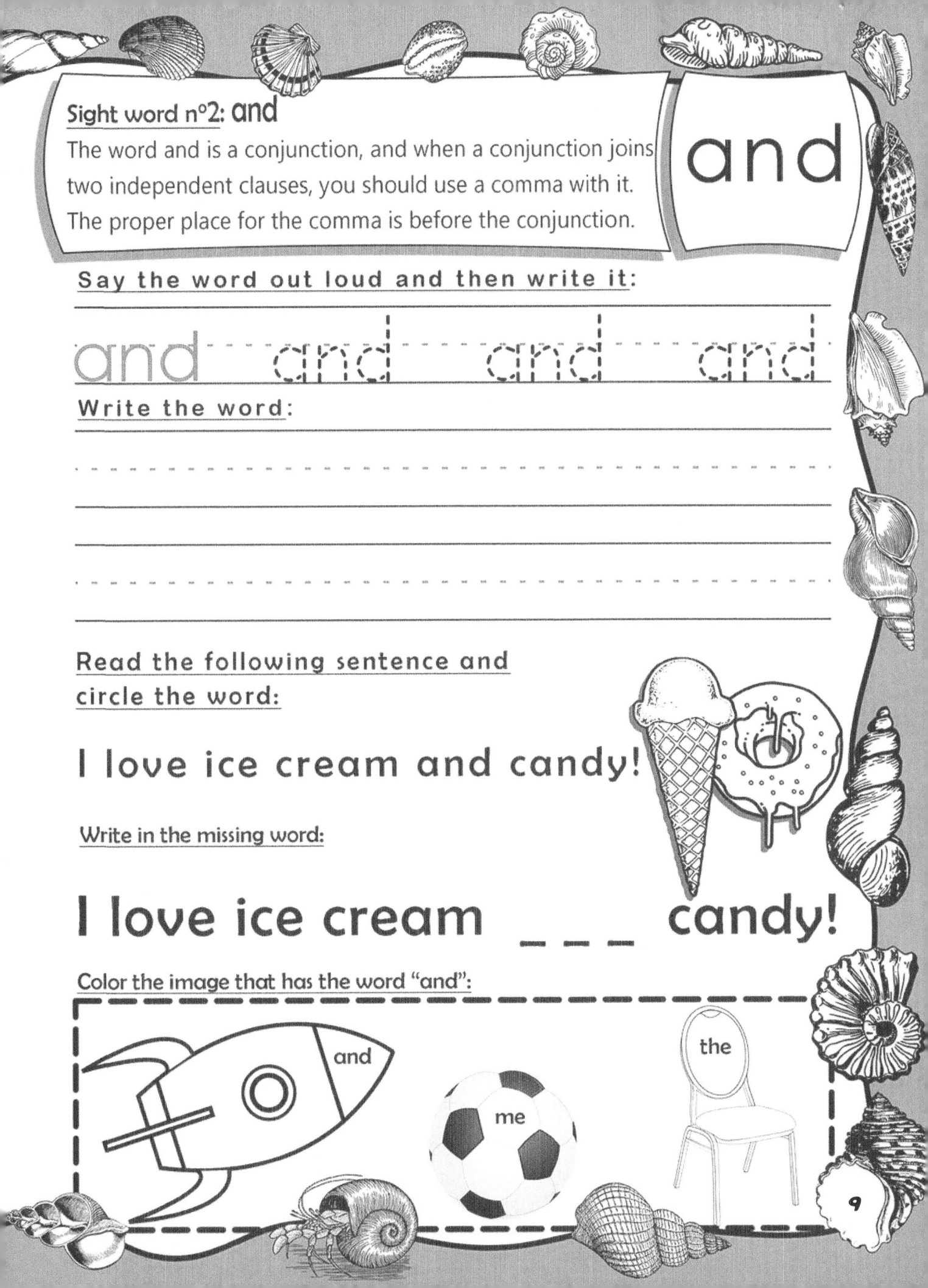

Say the word out loud and then write it:

and   and   and   and

Write the word:

Read the following sentence and circle the word:

I love ice cream and candy!

Write in the missing word:

I love ice cream ___ candy!

Color the image that has the word "and":

and   me   the

big

Sight word n°3: big
large or great in dimensions, bulk, or extent, and also large or great in quantity, number, or amountlarge or great in quantity, number, or amount

Say the word out loud and then write it:

big   big   big   big

Write the word:

....

....

....

Read the following sentence and circle the word:

T-rex is a big dinosaur!

Write in the missing word:

T-rex is a _ _ _ dinosaur!

Color the image that has the word "big":

for   him   big

Sight word n° 6: come

To move from a place thought of as "there" to or into a place thought of as "here".

come

Say the word out loud and then write it:

come   come   come

Write the word:

Read the following sentence and circle the word:

We are the first to come to school.

Write in the missing word:

We are the first to _____ to school.

Color the image that has the word "come":

who   cute   come

13

Sight word n° 7: **down**

down

- toward or in a lower physical position.
- to a lying or sitting position.
- toward or to the ground, floor, or bottom.

Say the word out loud and then write it:

down   down   down

Write the word:

Read the following sentence and circle the word:

He sat down at the table.

Write in the missing word:

He sat _ _ _ _ at the table.

Color the image that has the word "down":

down   plane   how

Sight word n° 10: **funny**
- affording light mirth and laughter.
- seeking or intended to amuse.

funny

Say the word out loud and then write it:

funny   funny   funny

Write the word:

Read the following sentence and circle the word:

This clown is funny!

Write in the missing word:

This clown is _ _ _ _ _ !.

Color the image that has the word "funny":

bee   Key   funny

17

Sight word n° 11: go

is used to explain that something or someone is moving away from where the speaker is now, or was, if used in the past form.

Say the word out loud and then write it:

go   go   go   go   go

Write the word:

Read the following sentence and circle the word:

I want to go home.

Write in the missing word:

I want to __ __ home.

Color the image that has the word "go":

cold   car   go

Sight word nº 12: help
- To aid or assist.
- To rescue or save.

help

Say the word out loud and then write it:

help   help   help   help

Write the word:

Read the following sentence and circle the word:

Help me do my homework!

Write in the missing word:

_ _ _ _ me do my homework!

Color the image that has the word "help":

help   drive   kids

19

here

Sight word nº 13: here

- Here means in this place.
- Here is defined as a way to express comfort, draw attention or announce presence.

Say the word out loud and then write it:

here ----- here ----- here

Write the word:

_____

_____

_____

Read the following sentence and circle the word:

Dad: "Jhon where are you?"   dad

Jhon: "I'm here dad".

Write in the missing word:

Dad: "Jhon where are you?"   Jhon

Jhon: "I'm _ _ _ _ dad".

Color the image that has the word "go":

white | here | take

Sight word n° 14: in

-in is defined as going from outside to inside.

in

Say the word out loud and then write it:

in   in   in   in   in   in

Write the word:

Read the following sentence and circle the word:

US chart.

I live in the United States.

Write in the missing word:

I live ___ the United States.

Color the image that has the word "in":

in

fun

for

21

Sight word n° 15: jump

-Jump is defined as to bounce or spring from the ground or from one surface to another.

Say the word out loud and then write it:

jump   jump   jump

Write the word:

Read the following sentence and circle the word:

The hare has a great ability to jump.

Write in the missing word:

The hare has a great ability to __ __ __ __ .

Color the object with the word "jump":

good   jump   green

Sight word n° 16: is

-The word "is" represents a singular form of the word be.

is

Say the word out loud and then write it:

is   is   is   is   is   is

Write the word:

Read the following sentence and circle the word:

Shaun the sheep is my favorite movie.

Write in the missing word:

Shaun the sheep __ my favorite movie.

Color the image that has the word "is":

from   is   Hello

little

Sight word nº 17: little
- little is small in size, quantity or importance.

Say the word out loud and then write it:

little   little   little

Write the word:

Read the following sentence and circle the word:

The little boy is intelligent.

Write the missing word:

The _ _ _ _ _ _ boy is intelligent.

Color the image that has the word "little":

him   little   run

Sight word n° 18: it

-The word "it" is used to represent an inanimate thing.

it

Say the word out loud and then write it:

it   it   it   it   it   it

Write the word:

Read the following sentence and circle the word:

I visited my uncle's farm,
It is a beautiful place.

Write in the missing word:

I visited my uncle's farm,
__ __ is a beautiful place.

Color the image that has the word "it":

sky   pig   it

25

look

Sight word n° 19: look

- Look means to turn one's eyes toward something or to gaze at something with the eyes.

Say the word out loud and then write it:

look   look   look   look

Write the word:

Read the following sentence and circle the word:

Look at this cute unicorn!

Write in the missing word:

_ _ _ _ at this cute unicorn!

Color the image that has the word "look":

look   have   black

26

Sight word n° 20: **me**
- me is defined as one's self when the speaker is referring to himself or herself.

me

Say the word out loud and then write it:

me   me   me   me   me

Write the word:

Read the following sentence and circle the word:

Give me a piece of cake.

Write in the missing word:

Give __ __ a piece of cake.

Color the object with the word "me":

bee   me   brown

27

Sight word n° 21: make
- to bring into being by building from separate parts.
- to create or produce.

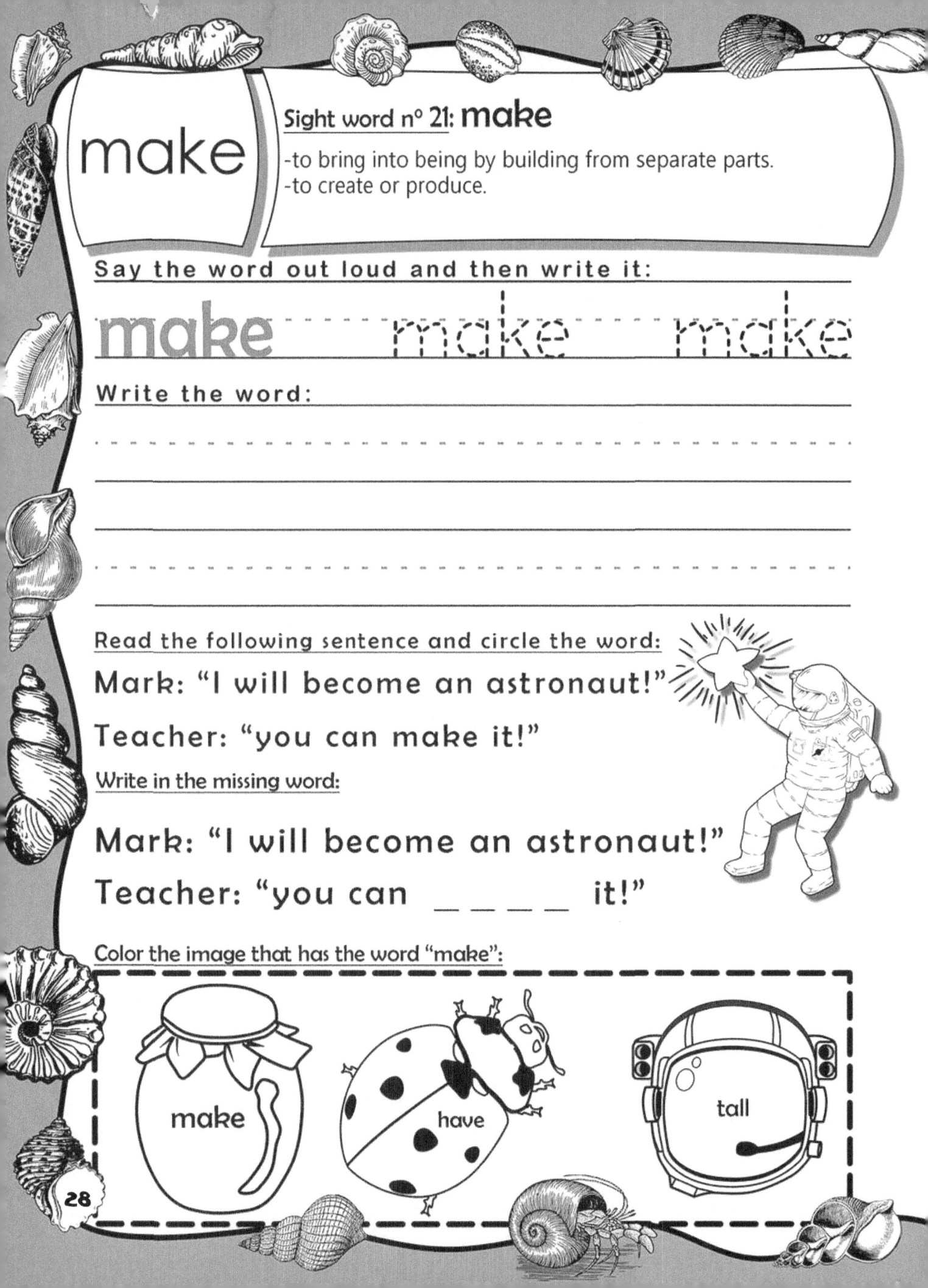

Say the word out loud and then write it:

make   make   make

Write the word:

Read the following sentence and circle the word:

Mark: "I will become an astronaut!"

Teacher: "you can make it!"

Write in the missing word:

Mark: "I will become an astronaut!"

Teacher: "you can _ _ _ _ it!"

Color the image that has the word "make":

make   have   tall

28

Sight word n° 22: my
- belonging to me, done by me, or having to do with me.

my

Say the word out loud and then write it:

my   my   my   my   my

Write the word:

Read the following sentence and circle the word:

This is my backpack.

Write in the missing word:

This is __ __ backpack.

Color the image that has the word "my":

my

yellow

good

not

Sight word n° 23: not
- in no way; to no degree; at no time.

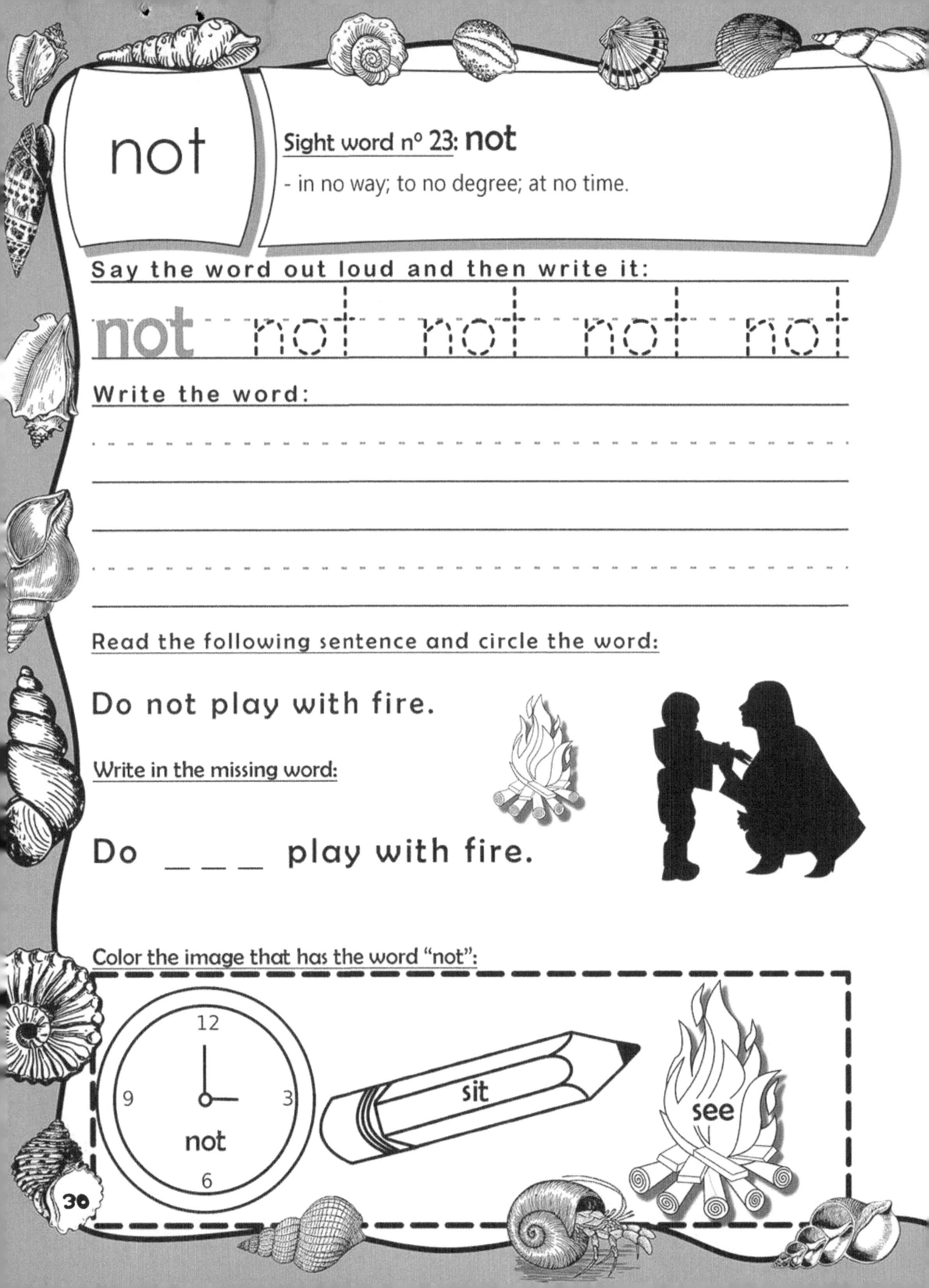

Say the word out loud and then write it:

not   not   not   not   not

Write the word:

Read the following sentence and circle the word:

Do not play with fire.

Write in the missing word:

Do ___ play with fire.

Color the image that has the word "not":

not   sit   see

30

Sight word n° 24: one

- being a single thing or person.
- united; not divided.
- at some future time, not named.

one

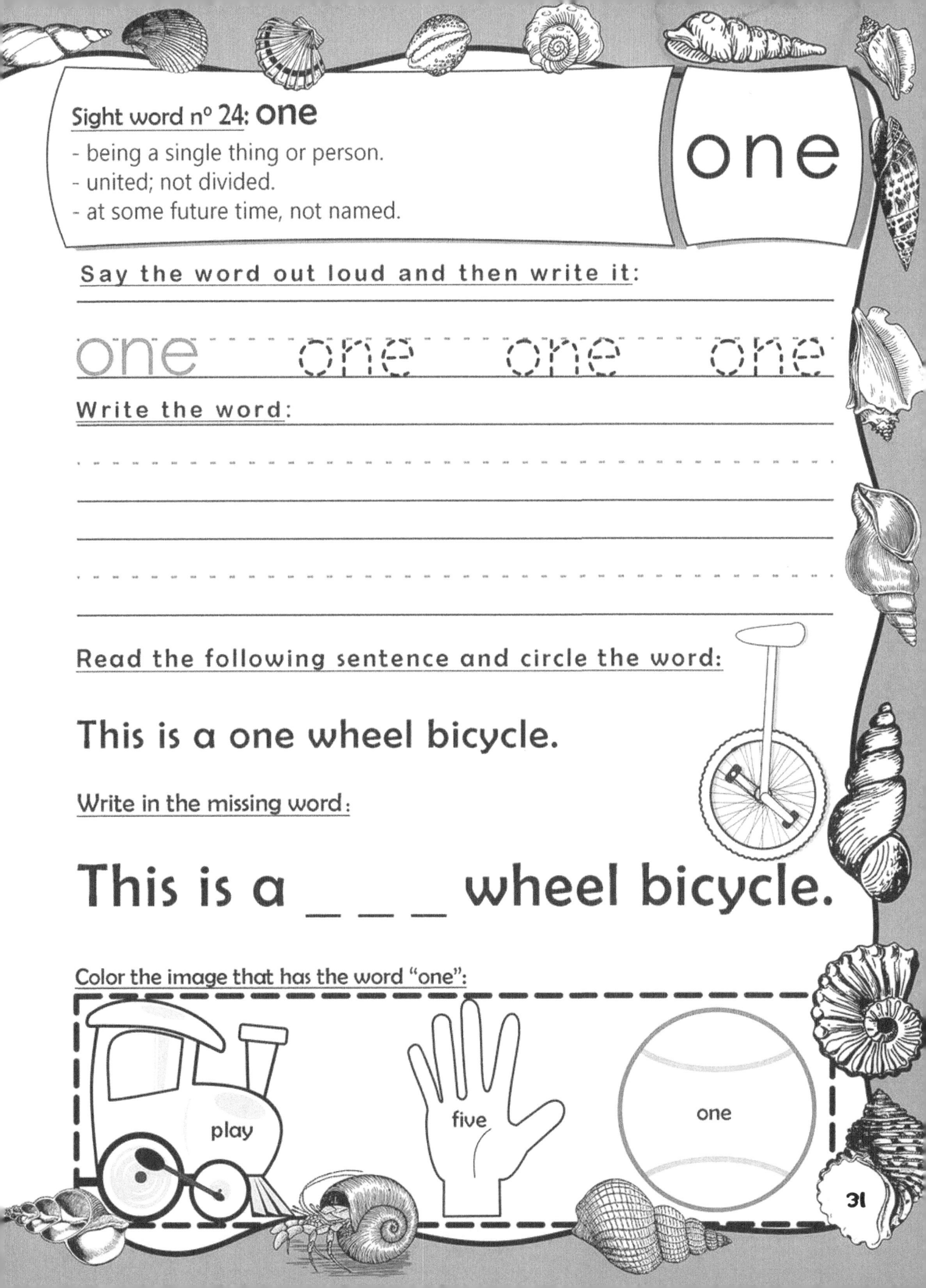

Say the word out loud and then write it:

one   one   one   one

Write the word:

Read the following sentence and circle the word:

This is a one wheel bicycle.

Write in the missing word:

This is a _ _ _ wheel bicycle.

Color the image that has the word "one":

play   five   one

play

Sight word n° 25: play

- An activity that is meant to relax or amuse.

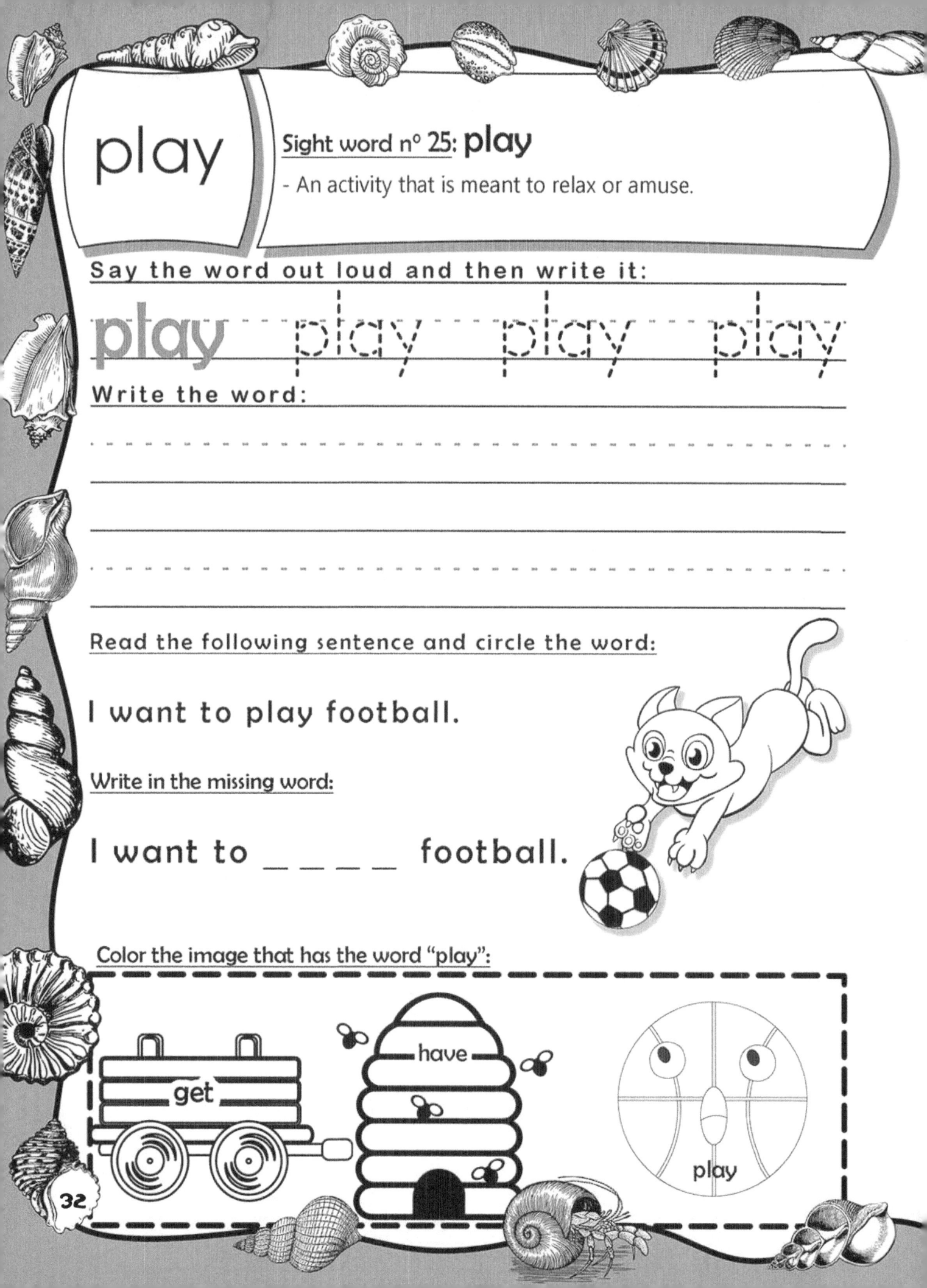

Say the word out loud and then write it:

play   play   play   play

Write the word:

Read the following sentence and circle the word:

I want to play football.

Write in the missing word:

I want to _ _ _ _ football.

Color the image that has the word "play":

get

have

play

32

Sight word n° 26: red
- the color of blood; the first color on the color spectrum.

red

Say the word out loud and then write it:

red   red   red   red

Write the word:

Read the following sentence and circle the word:

My blood color is red.

Write in the missing word:

My blood color is ___ .

Color the image that has the word "red":

go   red   light

run

Sight word n° 27: run

- to make oneself go forward by moving the legs very quickly.

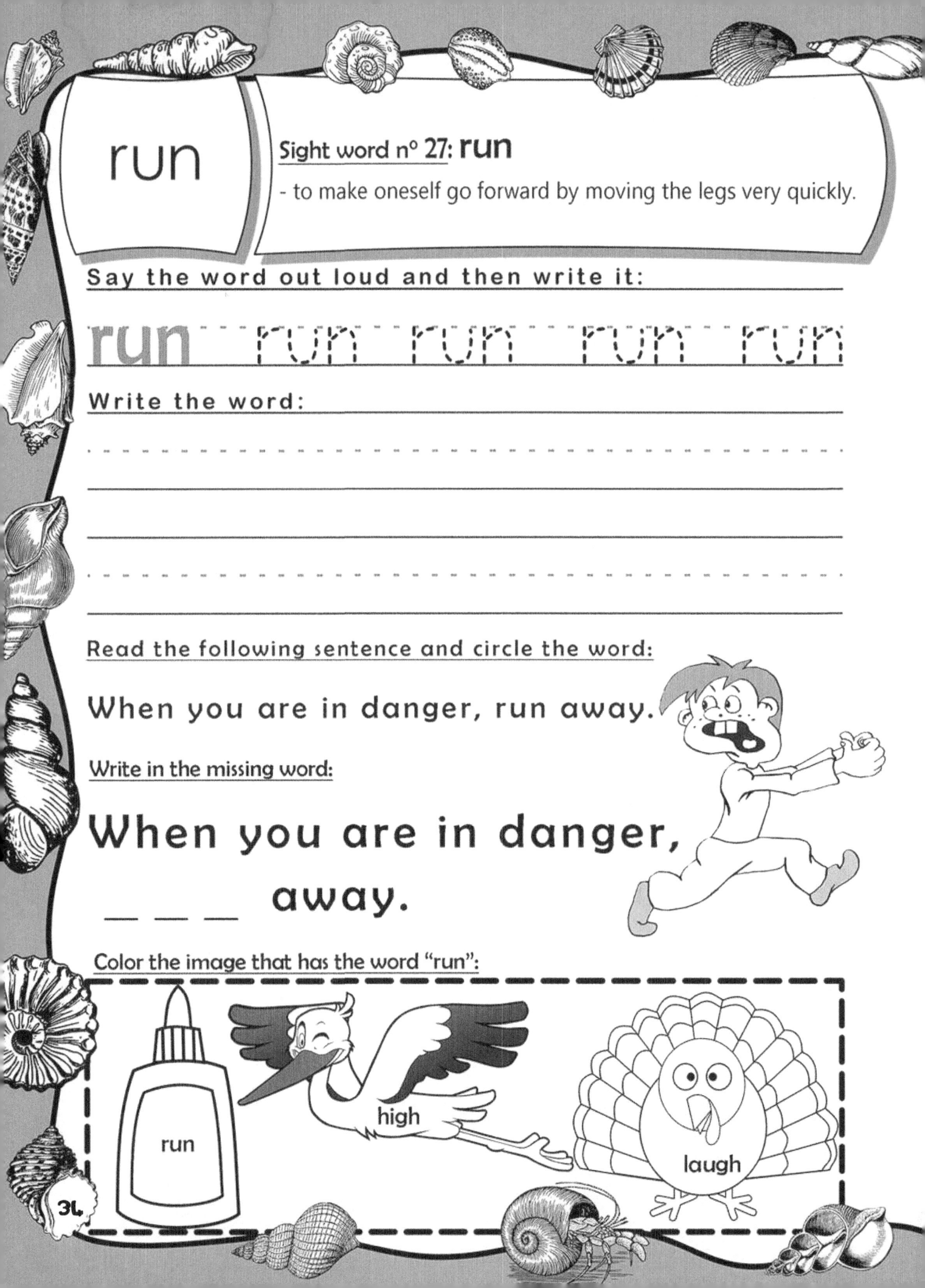

Say the word out loud and then write it:

run   run   run   run   run

Write the word:

Read the following sentence and circle the word:

When you are in danger, run away.

Write in the missing word:

When you are in danger, ___ away.

Color the image that has the word "run":

run   high   laugh

Sight word n° 28: **said**
- to produce (words or sounds) with one's voice.
- to express in speech or written words.

said

Say the word out loud and then write it:

said   said   said   said

Write the word:

Read the following sentence and circle the word:

In my letter, I said how much I love mom.

Write in the missing word:

In my letter, I _ _ _ _ how much I love mom.

Color the image that has the word "said":

said   try   run

35

see

Sight word nº 29: see
- to look at.

Say the word out loud and then write it:

see see see see see

Write the word:

Read the following sentence and circle the word:

Let's go and see the animals at the zoo.

Write in the missing word:

Let's go and _ _ _ the animals at the zoo.

Color the image that has the word "see":

who

high

see

Sight word nº 30: the
- used before a noun when the noun is something specific or already mentioned.

the

Say the word out loud and then write it:

the   the   the   the   the

Write the word:

Read the following sentence and circle the word:

I got the first rank in my class.

Write in the missing word:

I got ___ first rank in my class.

Color the image that has the word "the":

do   they   the

37

three

Sight word n° 31: three
- the number that comes after 2 and before 4 in the sequence of cardinal numbers; 3.

Say the word out loud and then write it:

three   three   three

Write the word:

_____

_____

_____

Read the following sentence and circle the word:

three rabbits.

Write in the missing word:

_ _ _ _ _ rabbits.

Write the missing letter:

thr_e   th_ee   thre_

t_ree   _hree

Sight word n° 32: to
- in the direction of; toward.
- as far as.

to

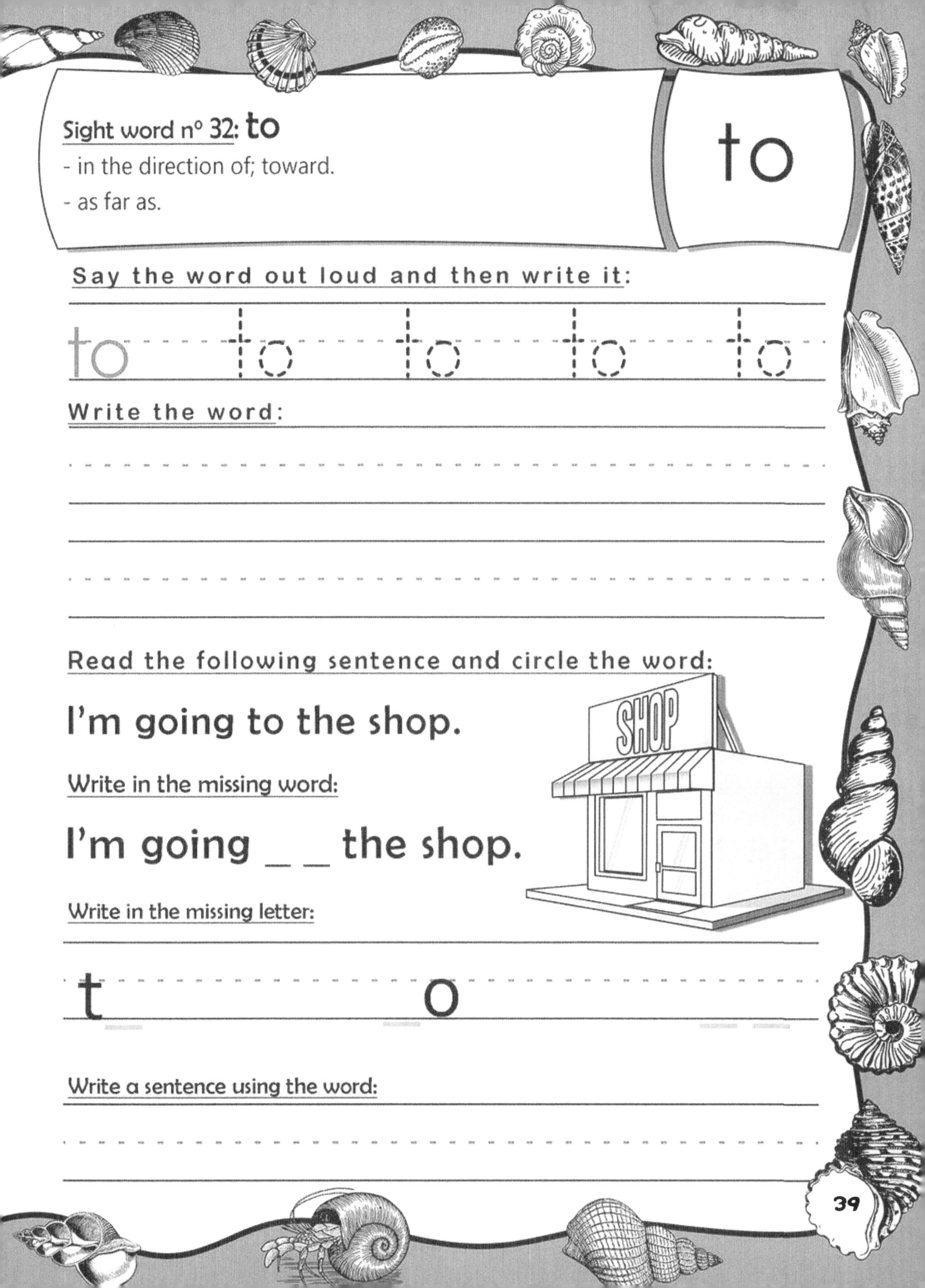

Say the word out loud and then write it:

to   to   to   to   to

Write the word:

Read the following sentence and circle the word:

I'm going to the shop.

Write in the missing word:

I'm going __ __ the shop.

Write in the missing letter:

t _   _ o

Write a sentence using the word:

39

two

Sight word nº 33: two
- the number that comes after one and before three in the sequence of cardinal numbers; 2.

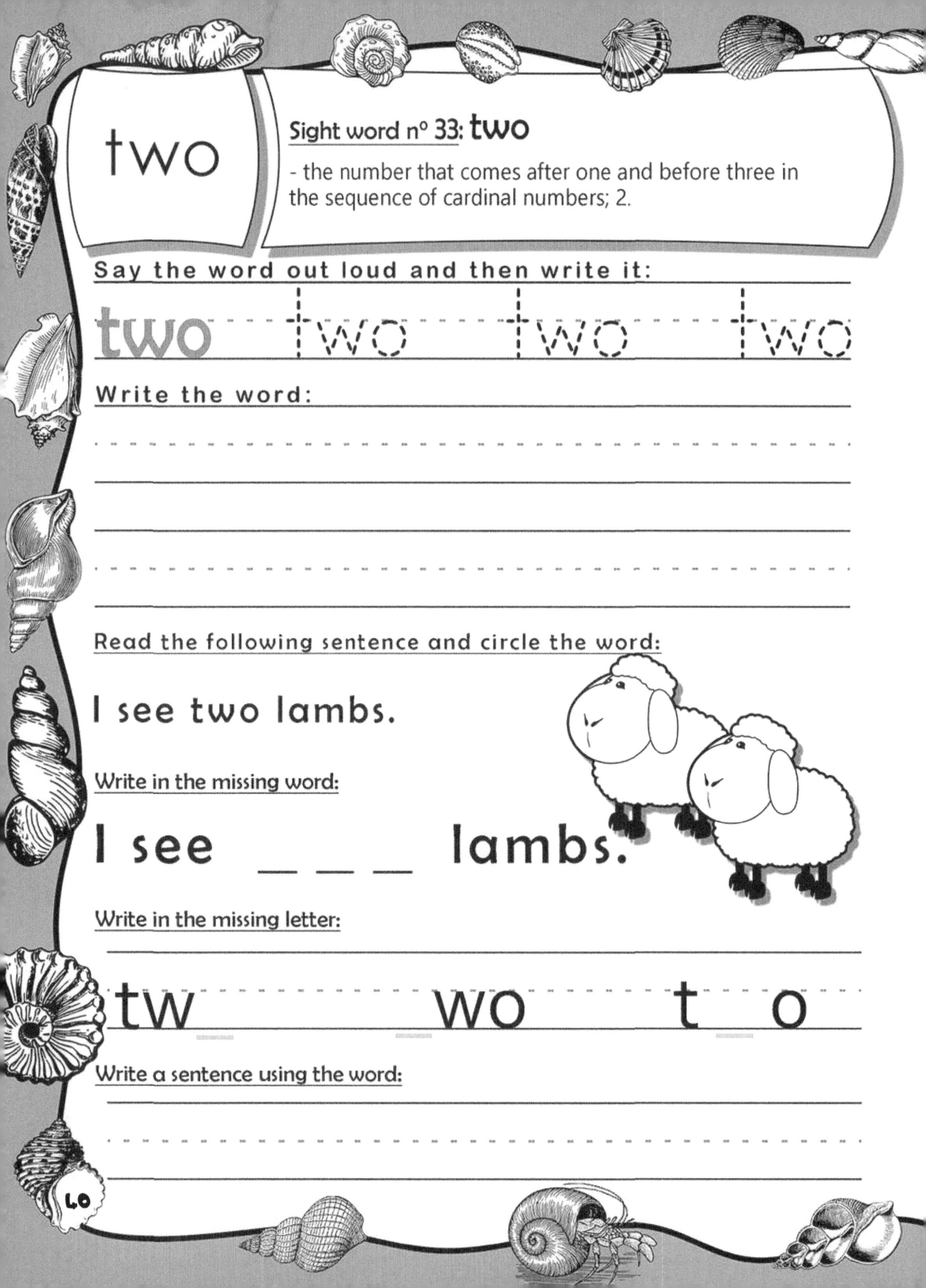

Say the word out loud and then write it:

two   two   two   two

Write the word:

Read the following sentence and circle the word:

I see two lambs.

Write in the missing word:

I see _ _ _ lambs.

Write in the missing letter:

tw_   _wo   t_o

Write a sentence using the word:

Sight word n° 34: up
- to, toward, at, or in a higher place or position.

up

Say the word out loud and then write it:

up   up   up   up   up

Write the word:

Read the following sentence and circle the word:

He gave me a thumbs up.

Write in the missing word:

He gave me a thumbs __ .

Write in the missing letter:

u _   _ p

Write a sentence using the word:

where

Sight word nº 35: where
- at, in, or to what location.
- in what position.

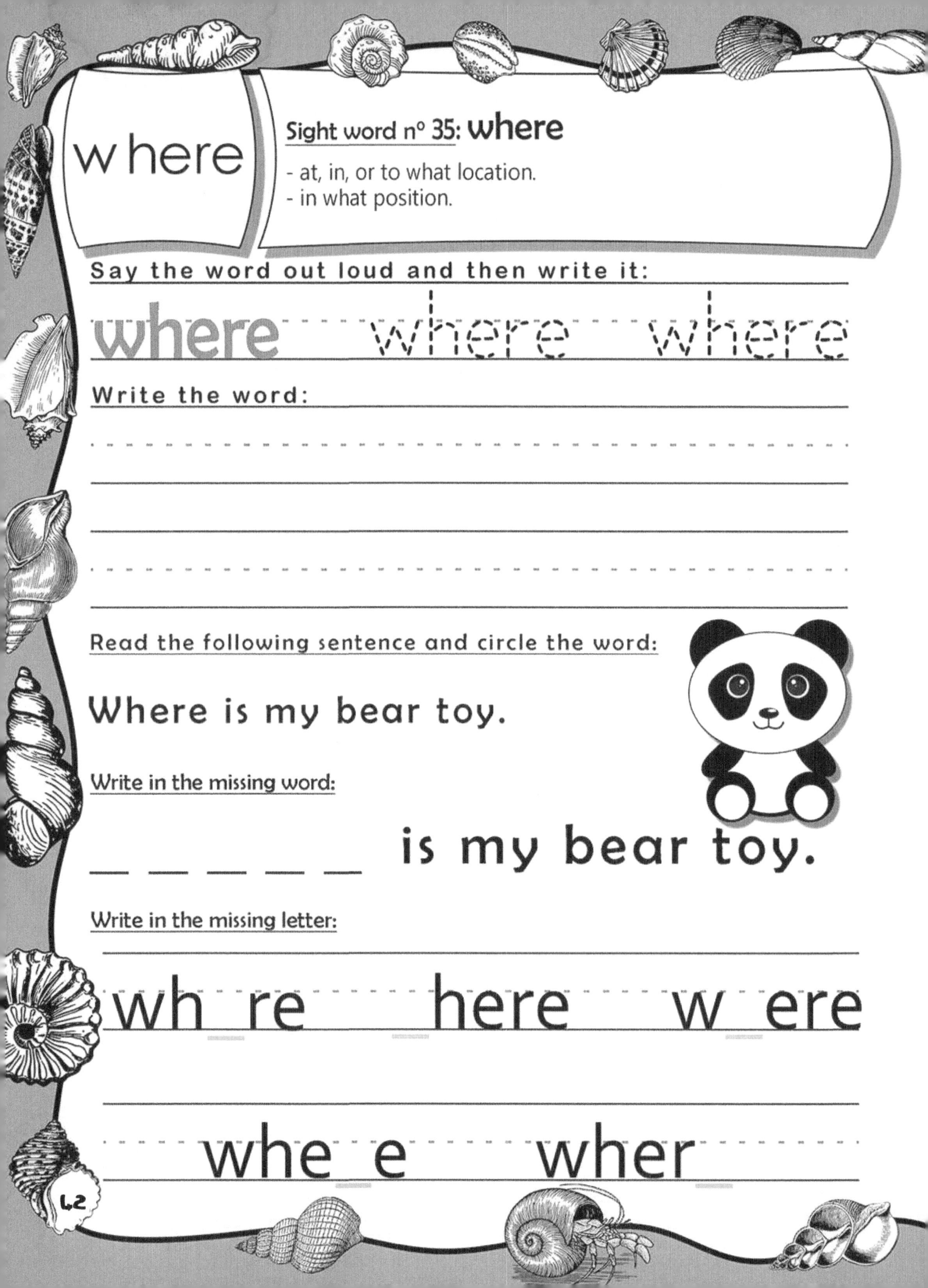

Say the word out loud and then write it:

where   where   where

Write the word:

Read the following sentence and circle the word:

Where is my bear toy.

Write in the missing word:

_ _ _ _ _ is my bear toy.

Write in the missing letter:

wh_re   _here   w_ere

whe_e   wher_

Sight word n° 36: **yellow**
- the color of an egg yolk or ripe lemon; the color between orange and green on the color spectrum.

yellow

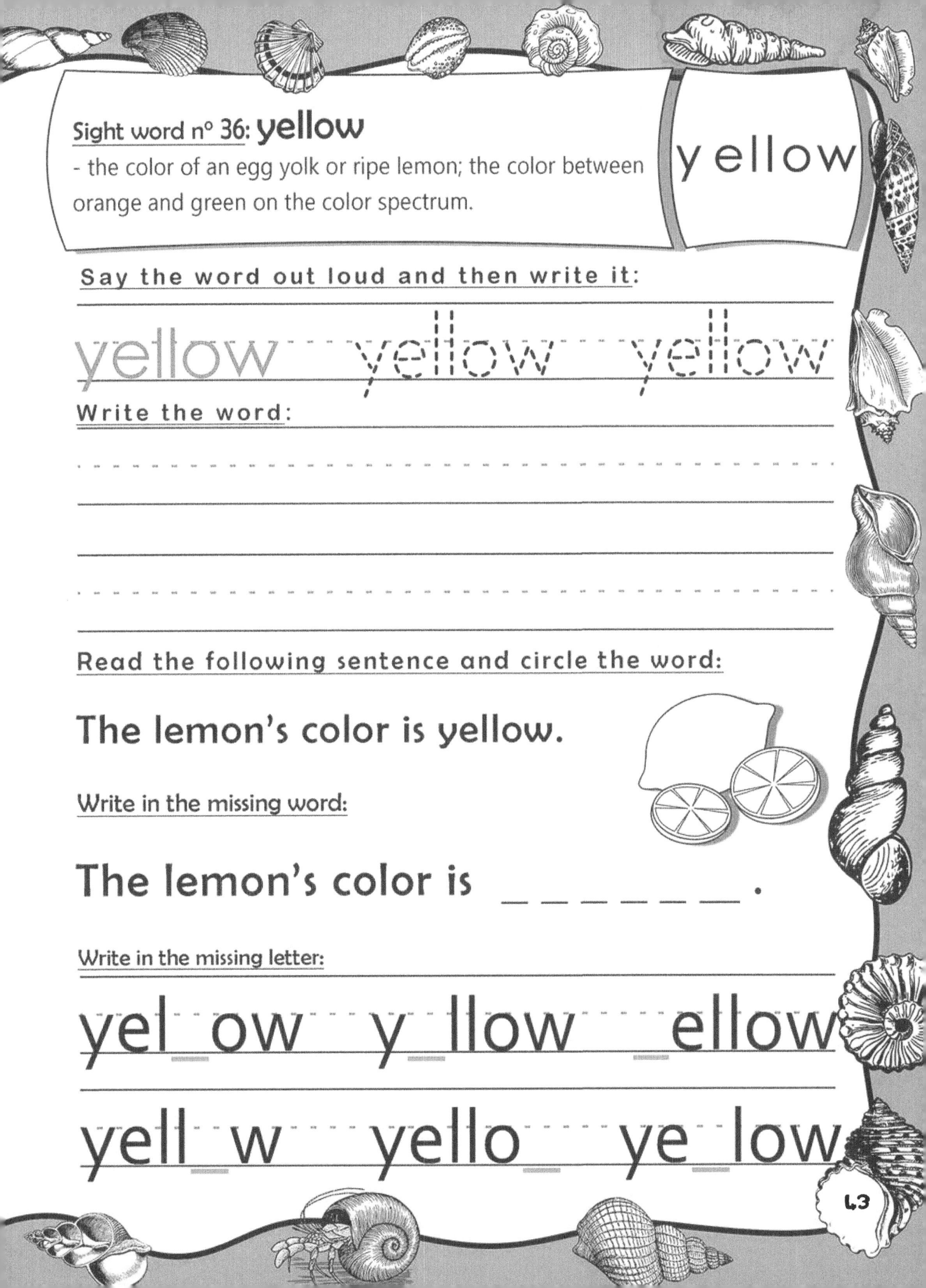

Say the word out loud and then write it:

yellow   yellow   yellow

Write the word:

Read the following sentence and circle the word:

The lemon's color is yellow.

Write in the missing word:

The lemon's color is _____ .

Write in the missing letter:

yel_ow   y_llow   _ellow

yell_w   yello_   ye_low

you

Sight word n° 37: you
- the person or persons being spoken or written to.

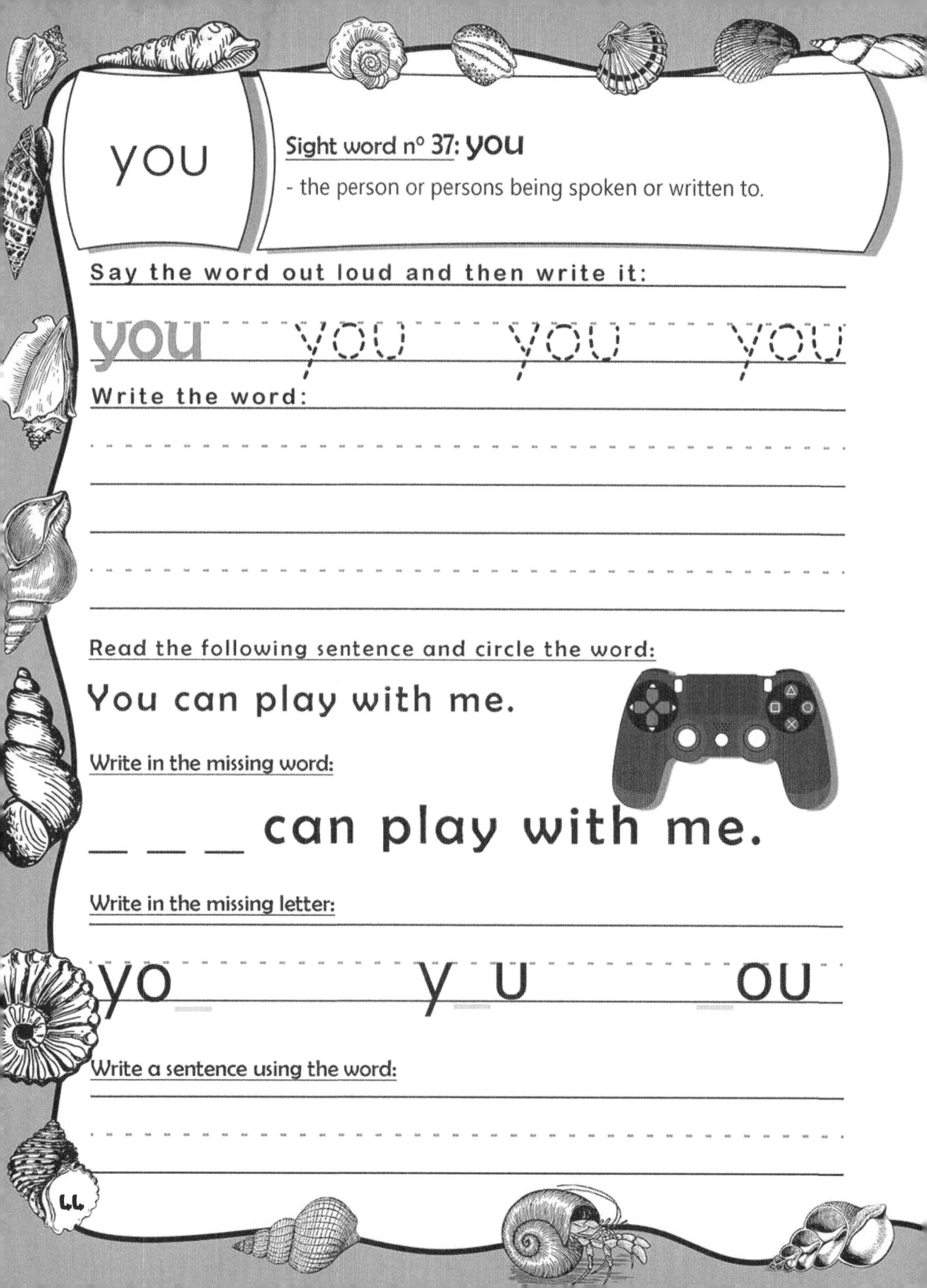

Say the word out loud and then write it:

you   you   you   you

Write the word:

Read the following sentence and circle the word:

You can play with me.

Write in the missing word:

___ can play with me.

Write in the missing letter:

yo_   y_u   _ou

Write a sentence using the word:

Sight word n° 38: **all**
- the whole of or every one of.
- a prefix that means in a complete or total way.

all

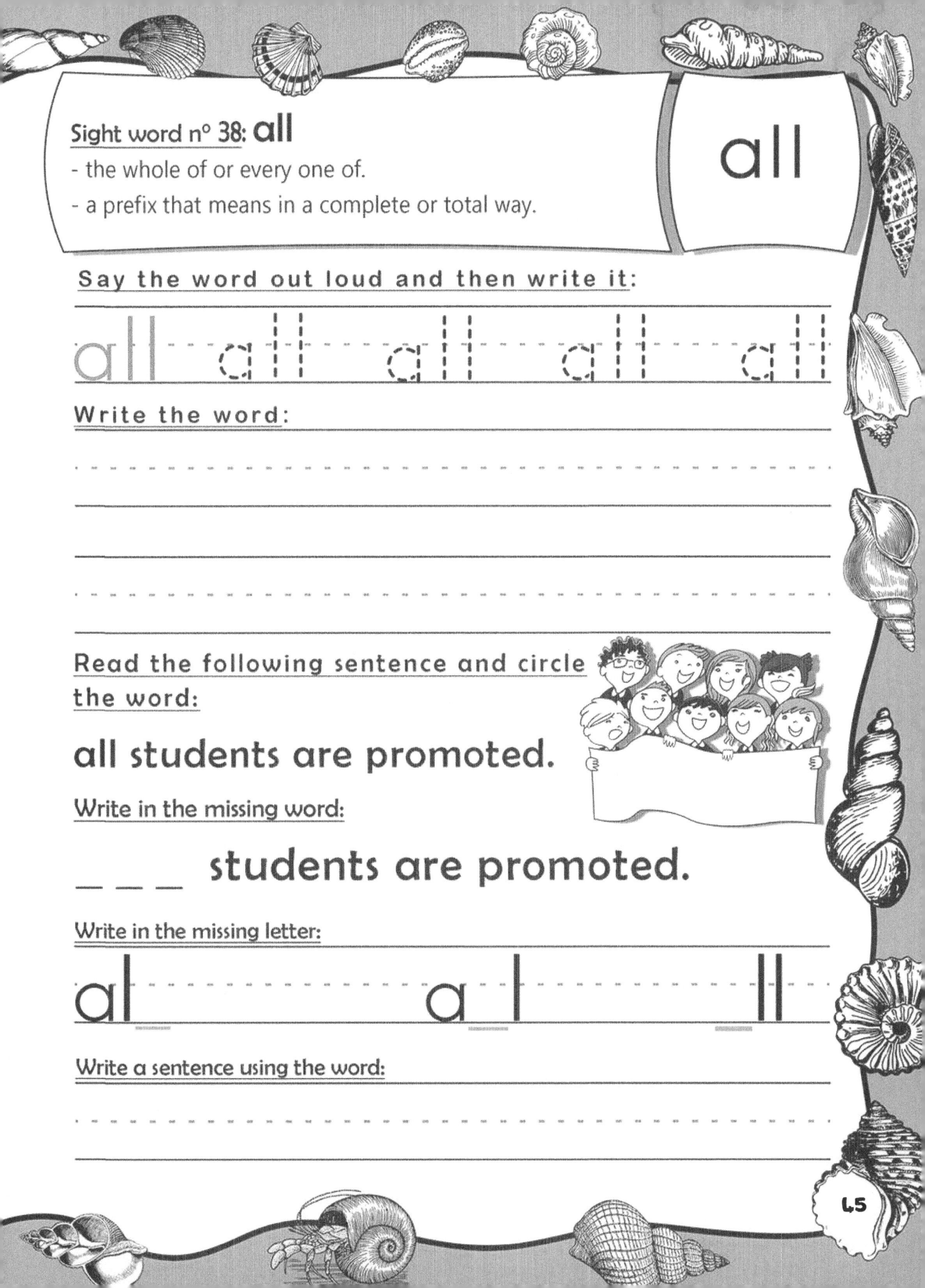

Say the word out loud and then write it:

all   all   all   all   all

Write the word:

Read the following sentence and circle the word:

all students are promoted.

Write in the missing word:

___ students are promoted.

Write in the missing letter:

al   a l   ll

Write a sentence using the word:

45

am

Sight word n° 39: am

- a form of the verb be that is present tense and used with the pronoun "I."

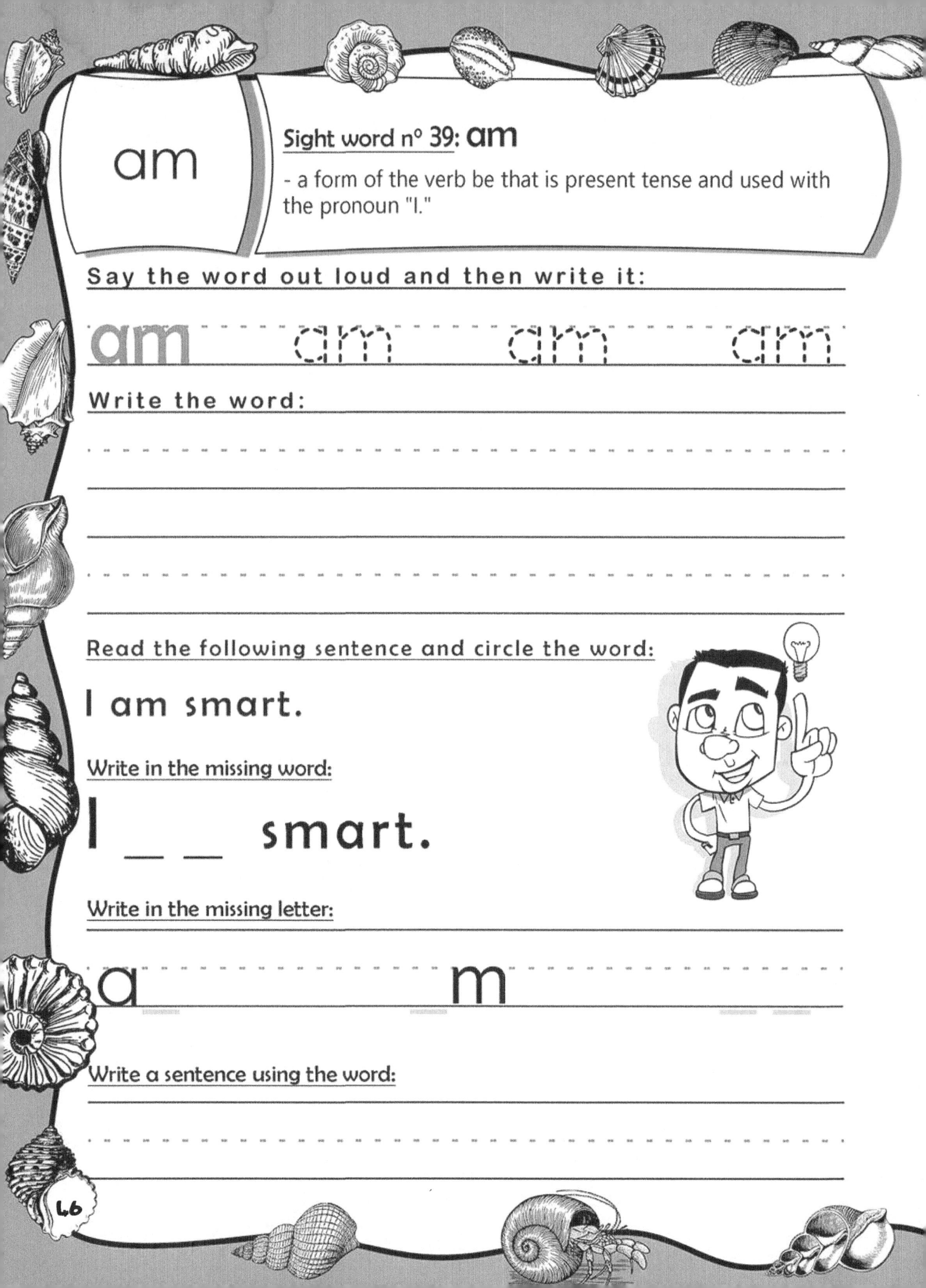

Say the word out loud and then write it:

am   am   am   am

Write the word:

Read the following sentence and circle the word:

I am smart.

Write in the missing word:

I _ _ smart.

Write in the missing letter:

a _____   _____ m

Write a sentence using the word:

Sight word n° 40: are

- a form of the verb be that is present tense and used with the pronouns "you," "we," or "they." It is also used with plural nouns.

are

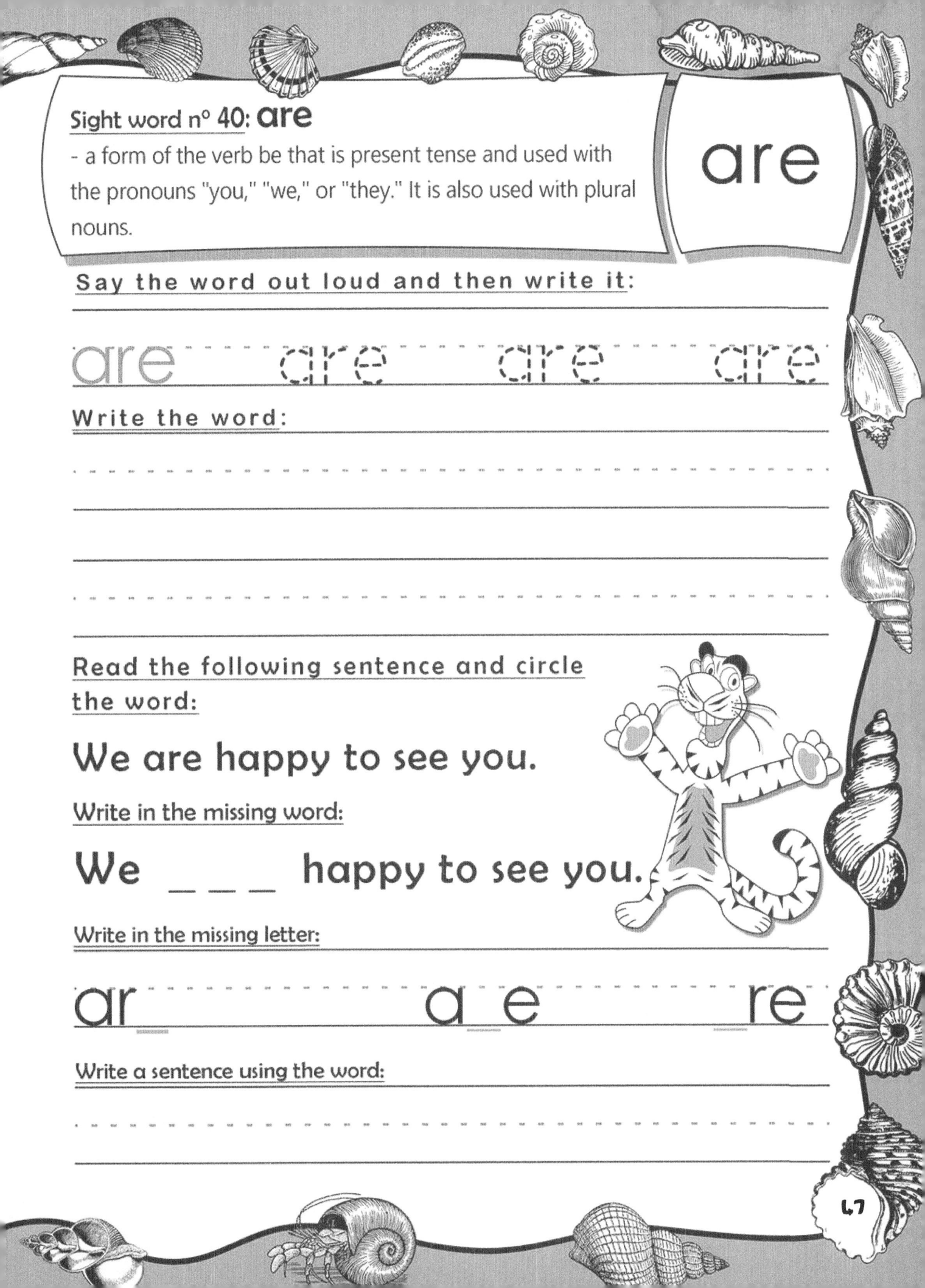

Say the word out loud and then write it:

are   are   are   are

Write the word:

Read the following sentence and circle the word:

We are happy to see you.

Write in the missing word:

We ___ happy to see you.

Write in the missing letter:

ar_   a_e   _re

Write a sentence using the word:

at

Sight word nº 41: at
- on or in the location of.

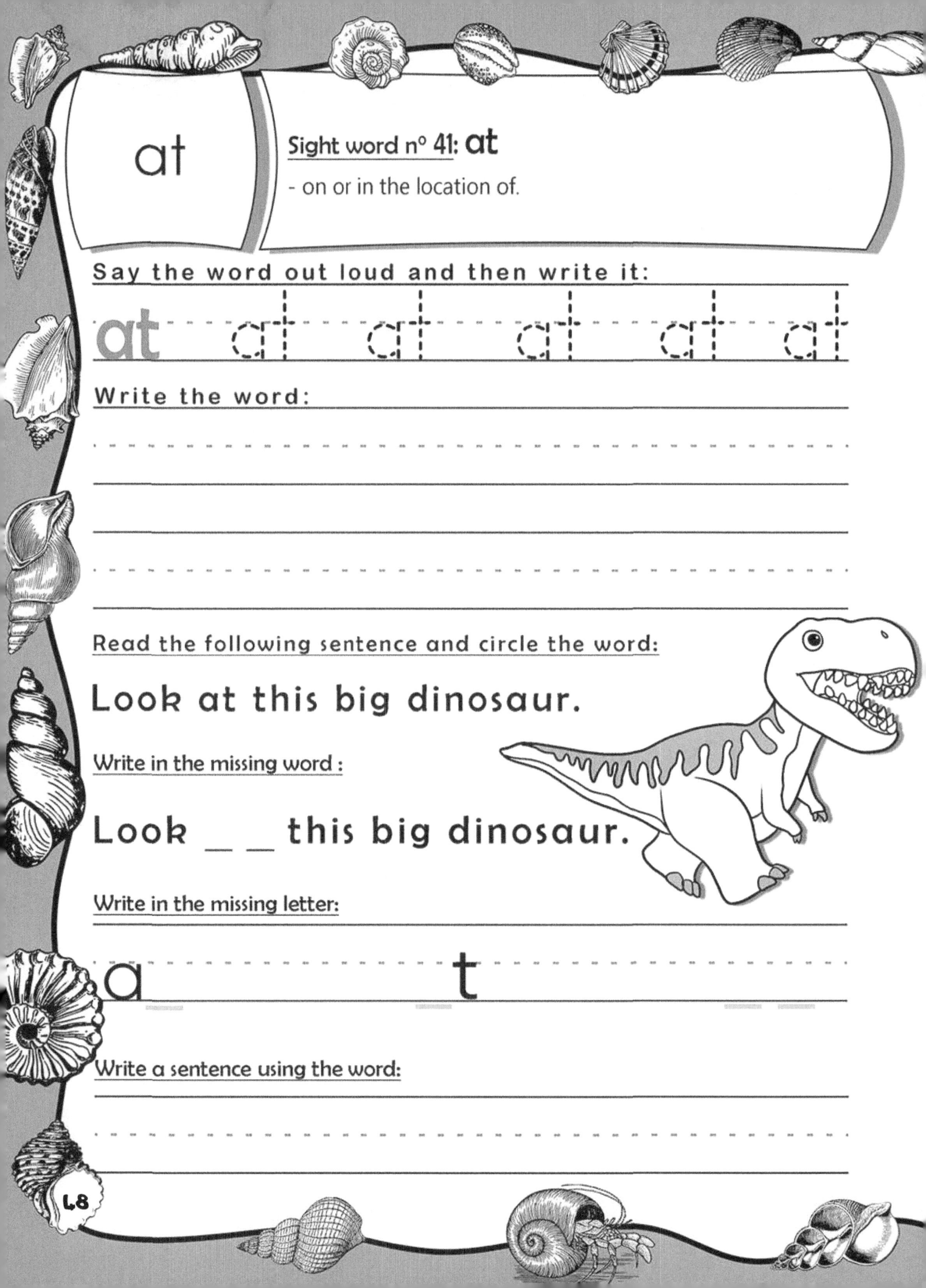

Say the word out loud and then write it:

at   at   at   at   at   at

Write the word:

Read the following sentence and circle the word:

Look at this big dinosaur.

Write in the missing word:

Look _ _ this big dinosaur.

Write in the missing letter:

a   t

Write a sentence using the word:

Sight word n° 42: **ate**
- to put into the mouth, chew, and swallow.

ate

Say the word out loud and then write it:

ate   ate   ate   ate

Write the word:

Read the following sentence and circle the word:

He ate his breakfast before he went to school.

Write in the missing word:

He ___ his breakfast before he went to school.

Write in the missing letter:

at___   a___e   ___te

Write a sentence using the word:

69

be

Sight word n° 43: be

- to live or exist.

Say the word out loud and then write it:

be be be be be be

Write the word:

Read the following sentence and circle the word:

I will be there on time.

Write in the missing word:

I will __ __ there on time.

Write in the missing letter:

b   e

Write a sentence using the word:

50

Sight word n° 44: **black**
- the color of the night sky; the darkest color.

black

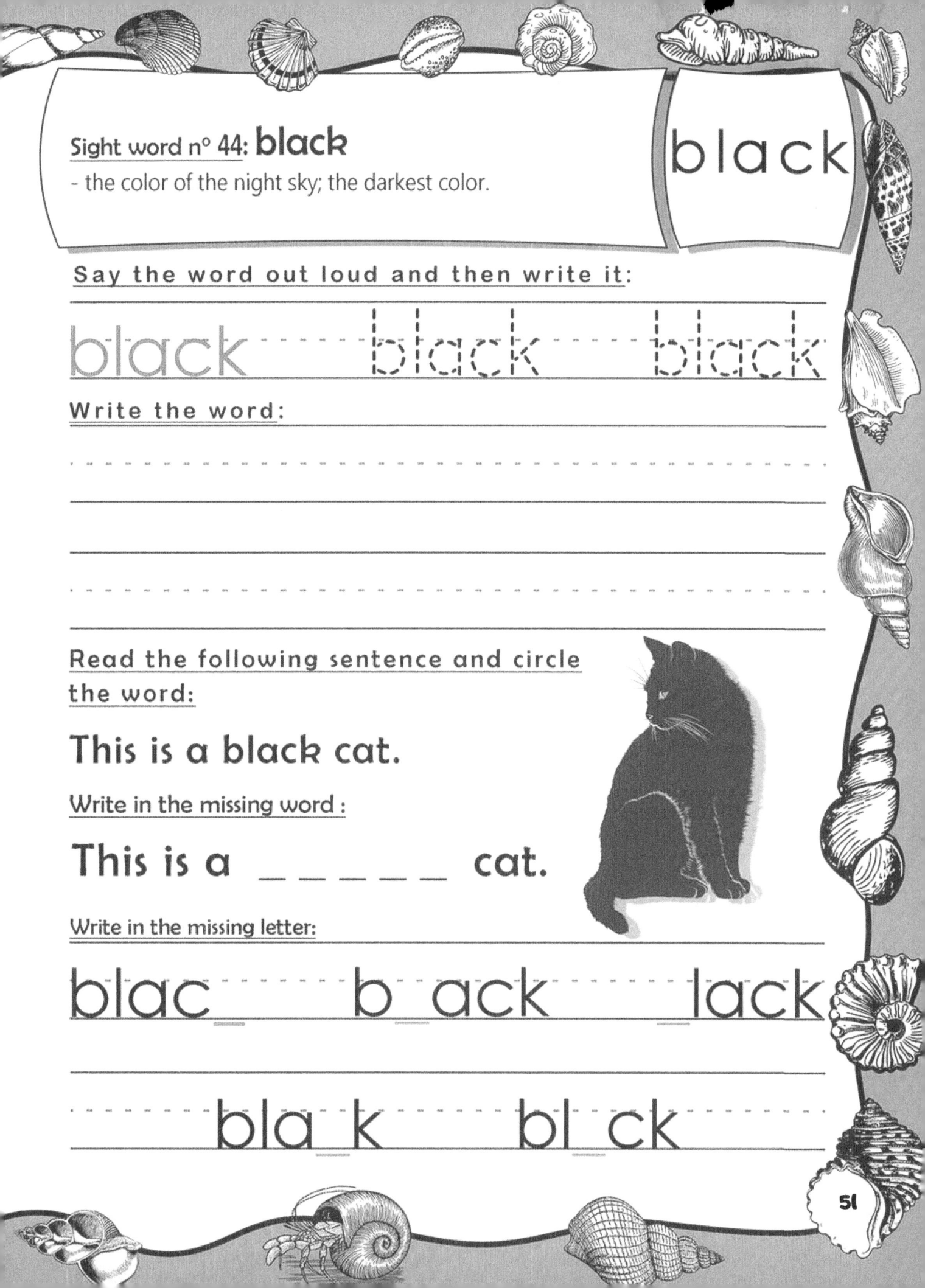

Say the word out loud and then write it:

black   black   black

Write the word:

Read the following sentence and circle the word:

This is a black cat.

Write in the missing word:

This is a _ _ _ _ _ cat.

Write in the missing letter:

blac___   b___ack   ___lack

bla___k   bl___ck

5l

but

Sight word nº 45: but
- in contrast; on the other hand.

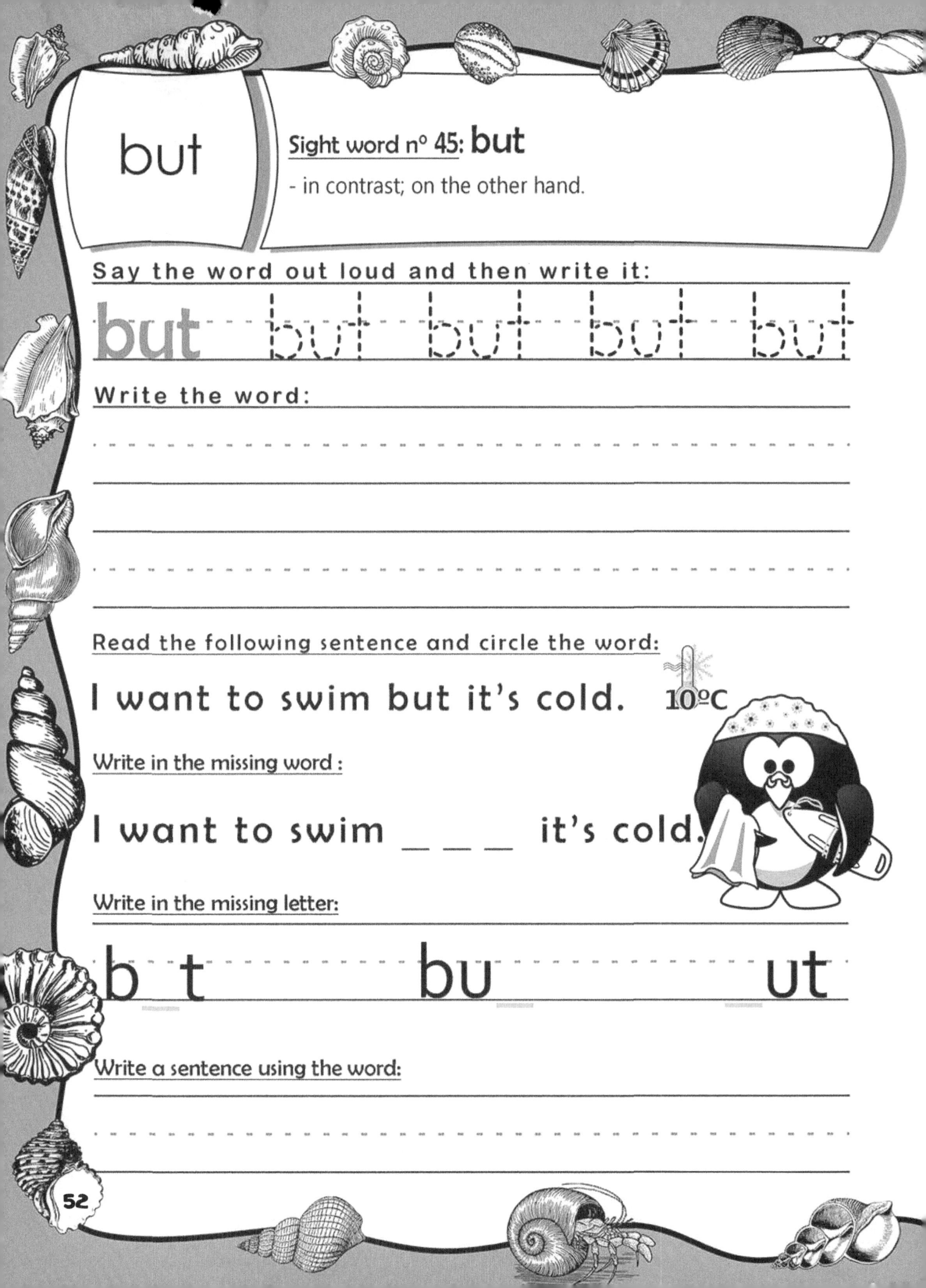

Say the word out loud and then write it:

but but but but but

Write the word:

Read the following sentence and circle the word:

I want to swim but it's cold.   10ºC

Write in the missing word:

I want to swim ___ it's cold.

Write in the missing letter:

b_t   bu_   _ut

Write a sentence using the word:

52

Sight word n° 46: **brown**
- the color that comes from mixing red, yellow, and black paint.

brown

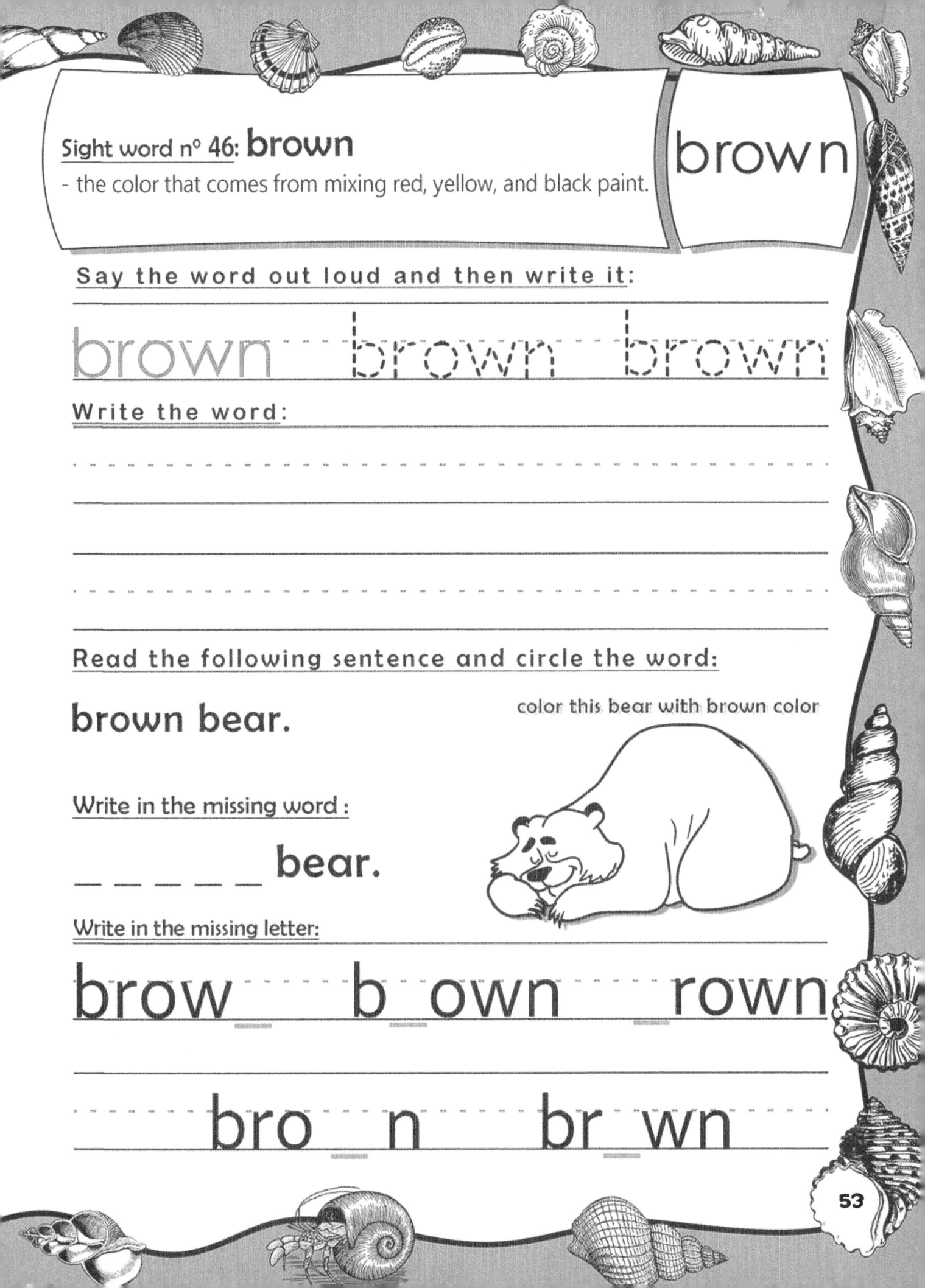

Say the word out loud and then write it:

brown   brown   brown

Write the word:

Read the following sentence and circle the word:

brown bear.

color this bear with brown color

Write in the missing word :

_ _ _ _ _ bear.

Write in the missing letter:

brow___   b_own   ___rown

___bro___n   br___wn

53

did

Sight word n° 47: did
- past tense of do.
- to carry out; perform.

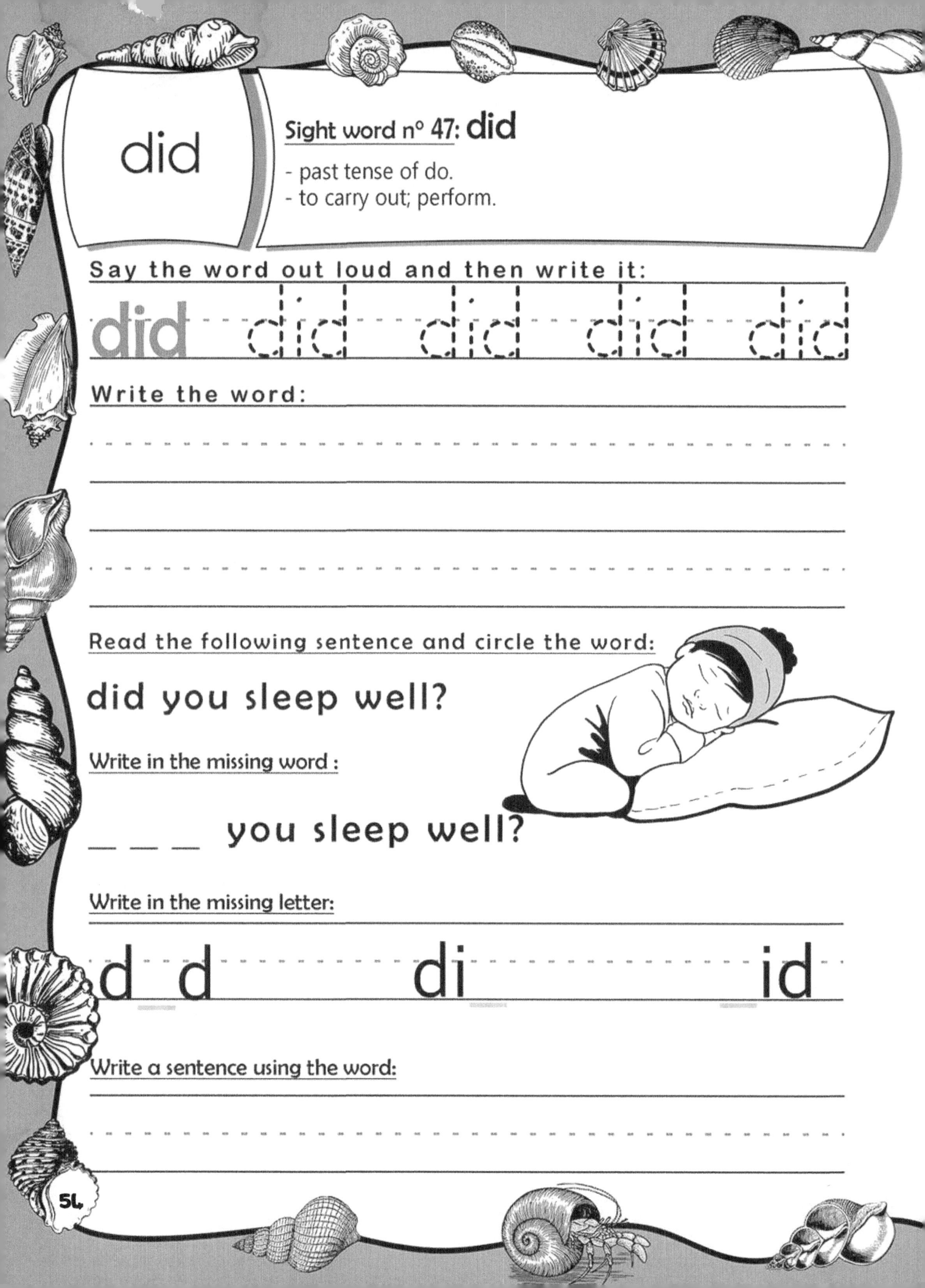

Say the word out loud and then write it:

did   did   did   did   did

Write the word:

....

_____

_____

....

_____

Read the following sentence and circle the word:

did you sleep well?

Write in the missing word:

_ _ _ you sleep well?

Write in the missing letter:

d _   _ d   d i _   _ _ id

Write a sentence using the word:

....

_____

Sight word n° 48: **came**
- past tense of come.
- to move or travel toward the speaker; approach.

came

Say the word out loud and then write it:

came   came   came

Write the word:

Read the following sentence and circle the word:

My friend came to visit me yesterday.

Write in the missing word:

My friend _ _ _ _ _ to visit me yesterday.

Write in the missing letter:

cam_   c_me   _ame

ca_e

do

Sight word n° 49: do
- to carry out; perform.

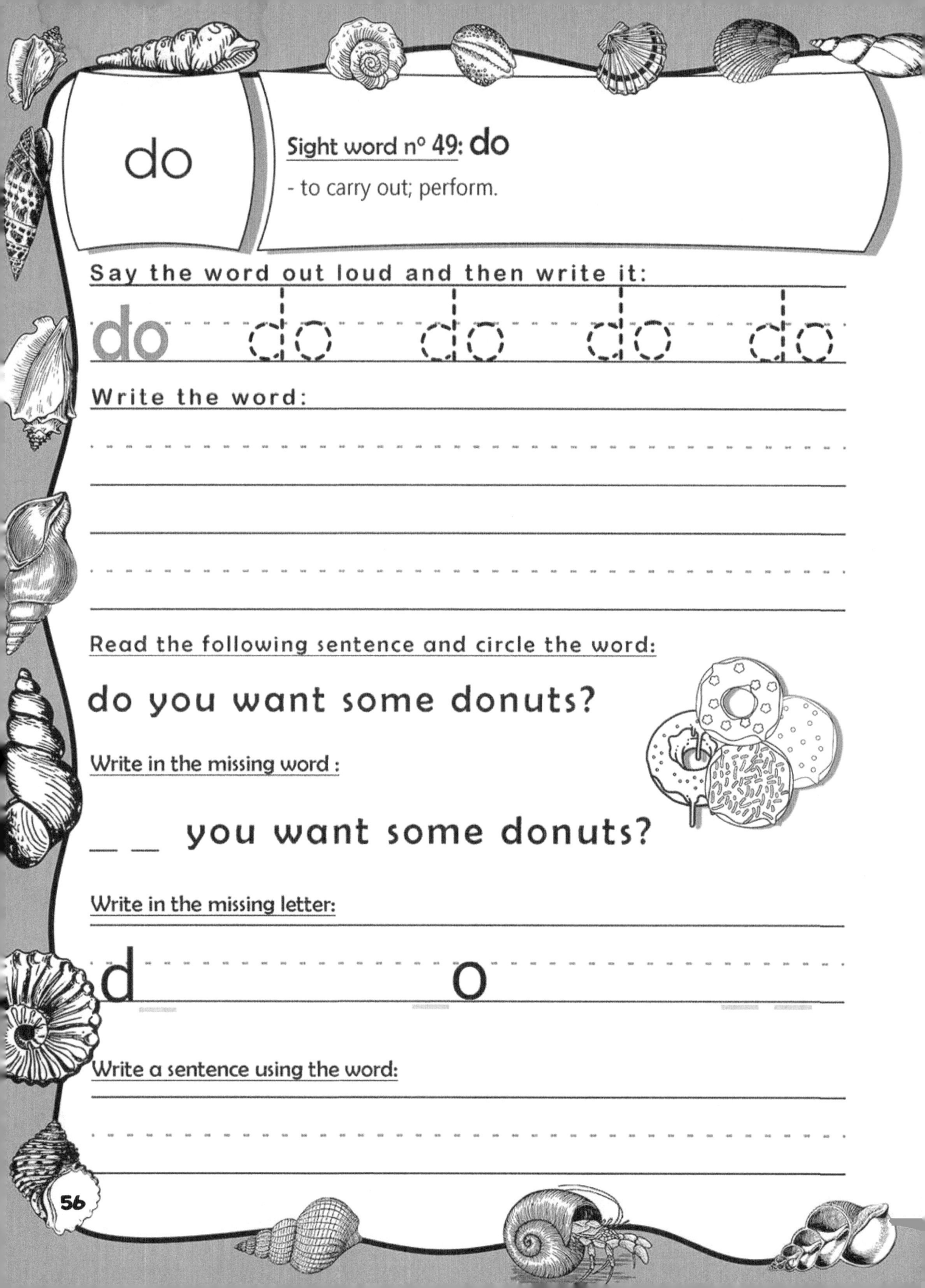

Say the word out loud and then write it:

do   do   do   do   do

Write the word:

Read the following sentence and circle the word:

do you want some donuts?

Write in the missing word :

__ you want some donuts?

Write in the missing letter:

d   o

Write a sentence using the word:

Sight word n° 50: **eat**
- to put into the mouth, chew, and swallow.

eat

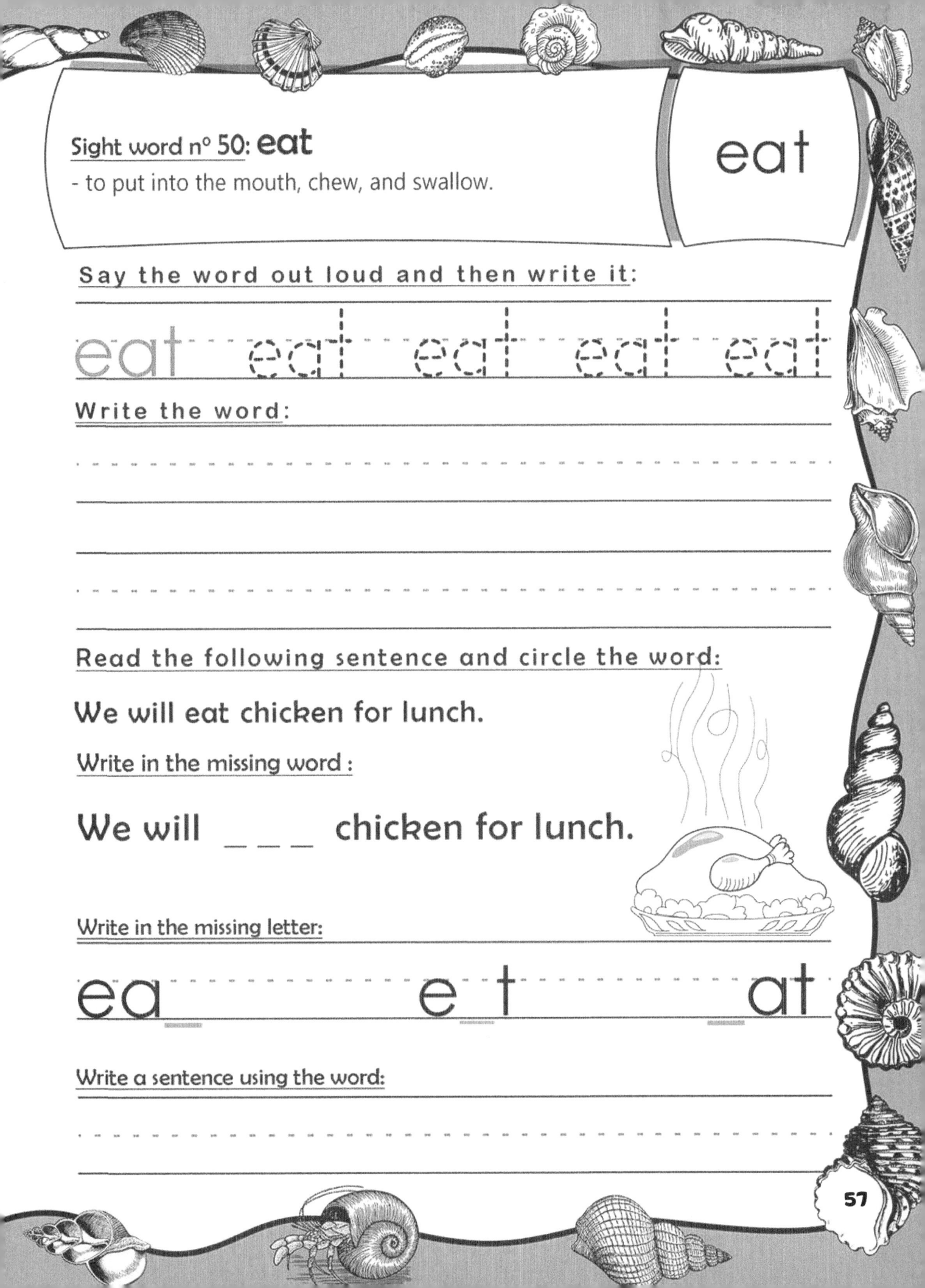

Say the word out loud and then write it:

eat   eat   eat   eat   eat

Write the word:

_____

_____

_____

Read the following sentence and circle the word:

We will eat chicken for lunch.

Write in the missing word:

We will ___ chicken for lunch.

Write in the missing letter:

ea___   ___e t   ___at

Write a sentence using the word:

_____

_____

four

Sight word n° 51: four
- the number that comes after 3 and before 5 in the sequence of cardinal numbers; 4.

Say the word out loud and then write it:

four   four   four   four

Write the word:

Read the following sentence and circle the word:

I have four pens.

Write in the missing word :

I have _ _ _ _ pens?

Write in the missing letter:

fou___   ___our   fo___r

f___ur

Write a sentence using the word:

58

Sight word n° 52: **get**
- to receive; come to have; gain; acquire.

get

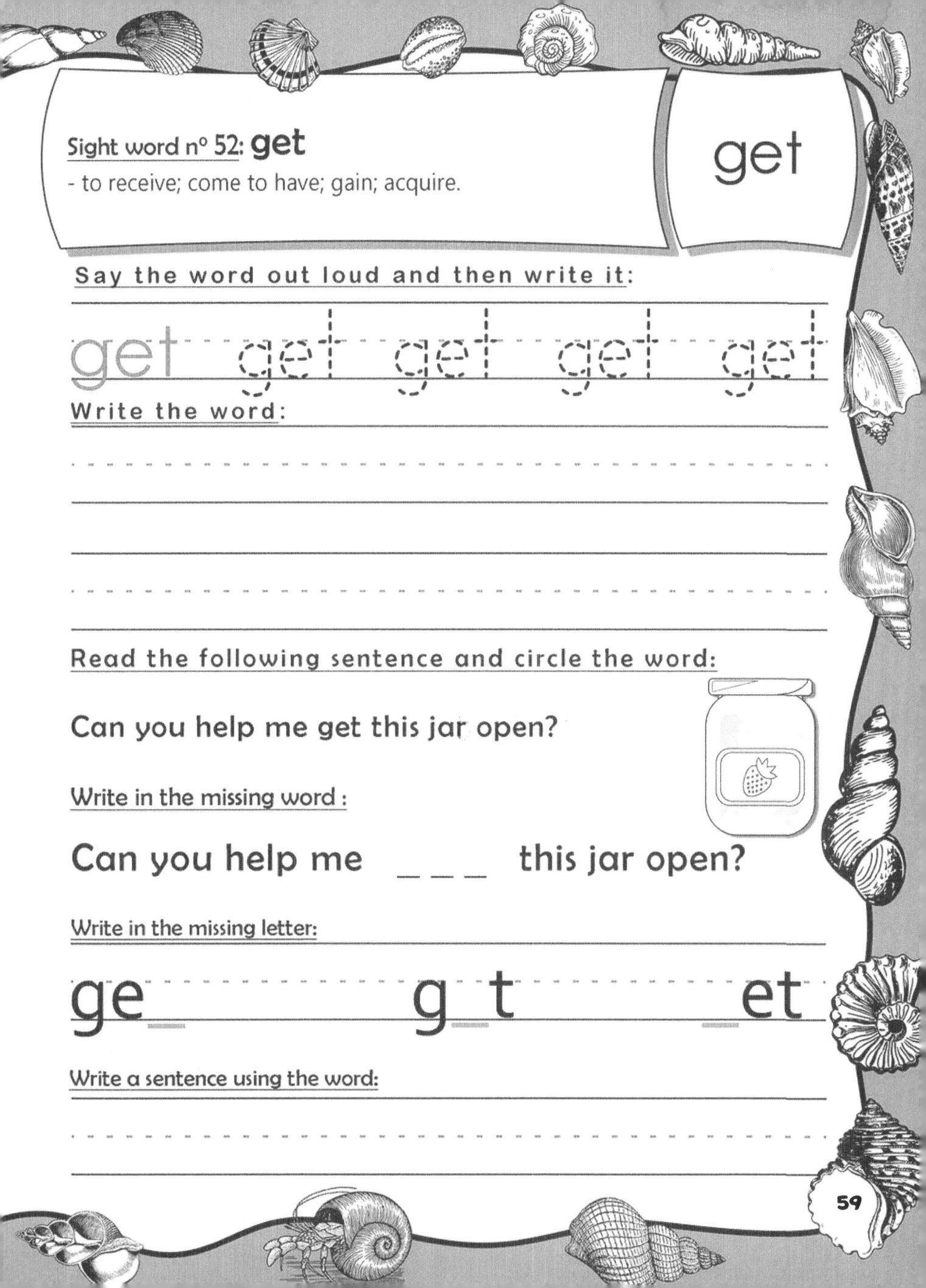

Say the word out loud and then write it:

get   get   get   get   get

Write the word:

Read the following sentence and circle the word:

Can you help me get this jar open?

Write in the missing word:

Can you help me ___ this jar open?

Write in the missing letter:

ge__   g_t   __et

Write a sentence using the word:

59

good

Sight word nº 53: good
- having qualities that are desired.

Say the word out loud and then write it:

good   good   good

Write the word:

_____

Read the following sentence and circle the word:

It was a good game.

Write in the missing word :

It was a _good_ game?

Write in the missing letter:

goo___   ___ood   go___d

g___od

Write a sentence using the word:

_____

Sight word n° 54: **he**
- the male human being or animal that is being discussed or was recently referred to.

he

Say the word out loud and then write it:

he   he   he   he   he

Write the word:

he   he   he   he   he

he he hehe hehe he

Read the following sentence and circle the word:

He is very fast.

Write in the missing :

He is very fast.

Write in the missing letter:

he   he   he

Write a sentence using the word:

he is very good

have

Sight word n° 55: have
- to own; possess.

Say the word out loud and then write it:

have   have   have

Write the word:

_____

_____

Read the following sentence and circle the word:

I have a lot of toys.

Write in the missing word:

I _____ a lot of toys.

Write in the missing letter:

hav_   _ave   ha_e

h_ve

Write a sentence using the word:

_____

_____

Sight word n° 56: **into**
- to the inside of.

into

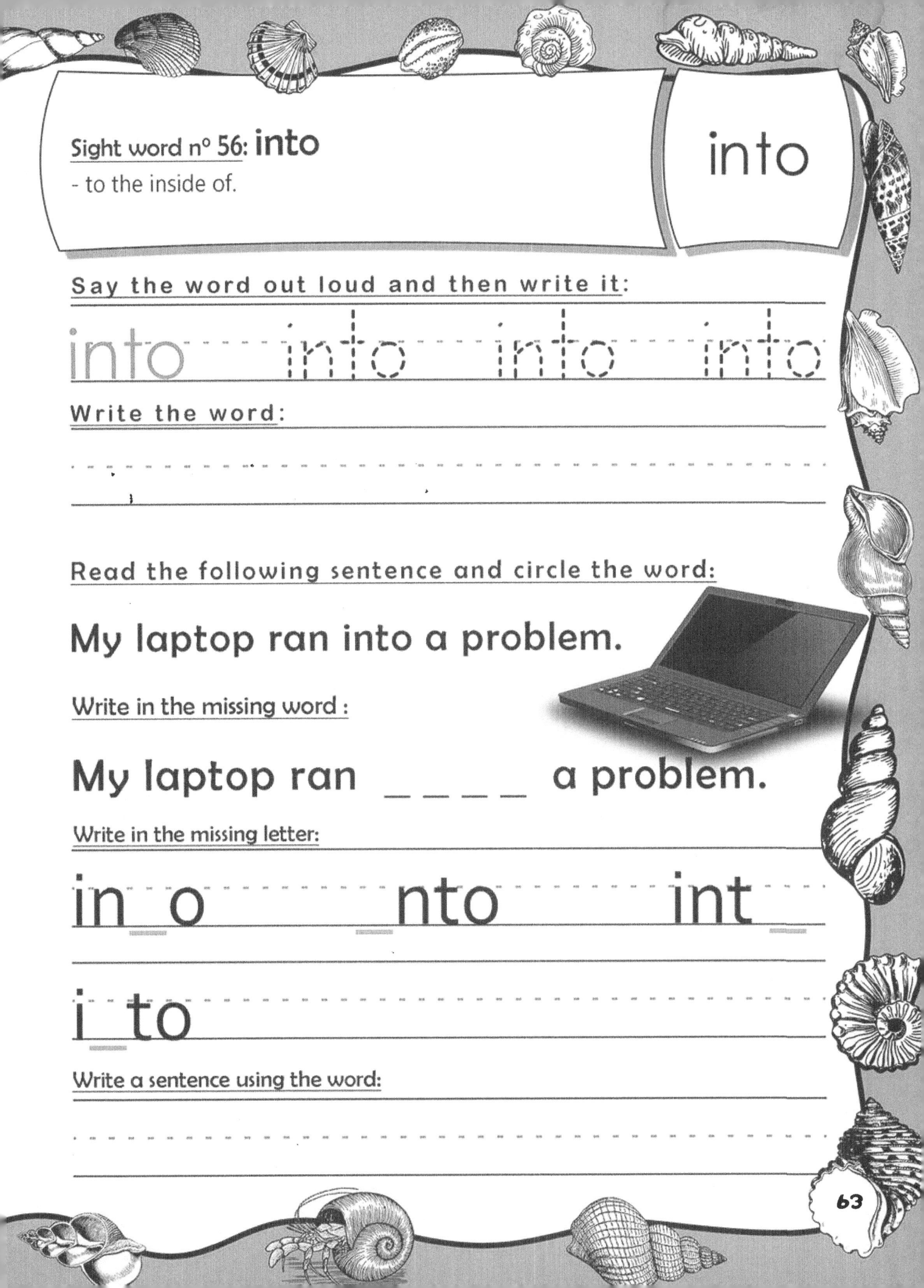

Say the word out loud and then write it:

into   into   into   into

Write the word:

_____

Read the following sentence and circle the word:

My laptop ran into a problem.

Write in the missing word :

My laptop ran ____ a problem.

Write in the missing letter:

in_o   _nto   int_

i_to

Write a sentence using the word:

_____

63

like

Sight word nº 57: like
- having close resemblance.
- to find pleasure in; enjoy.

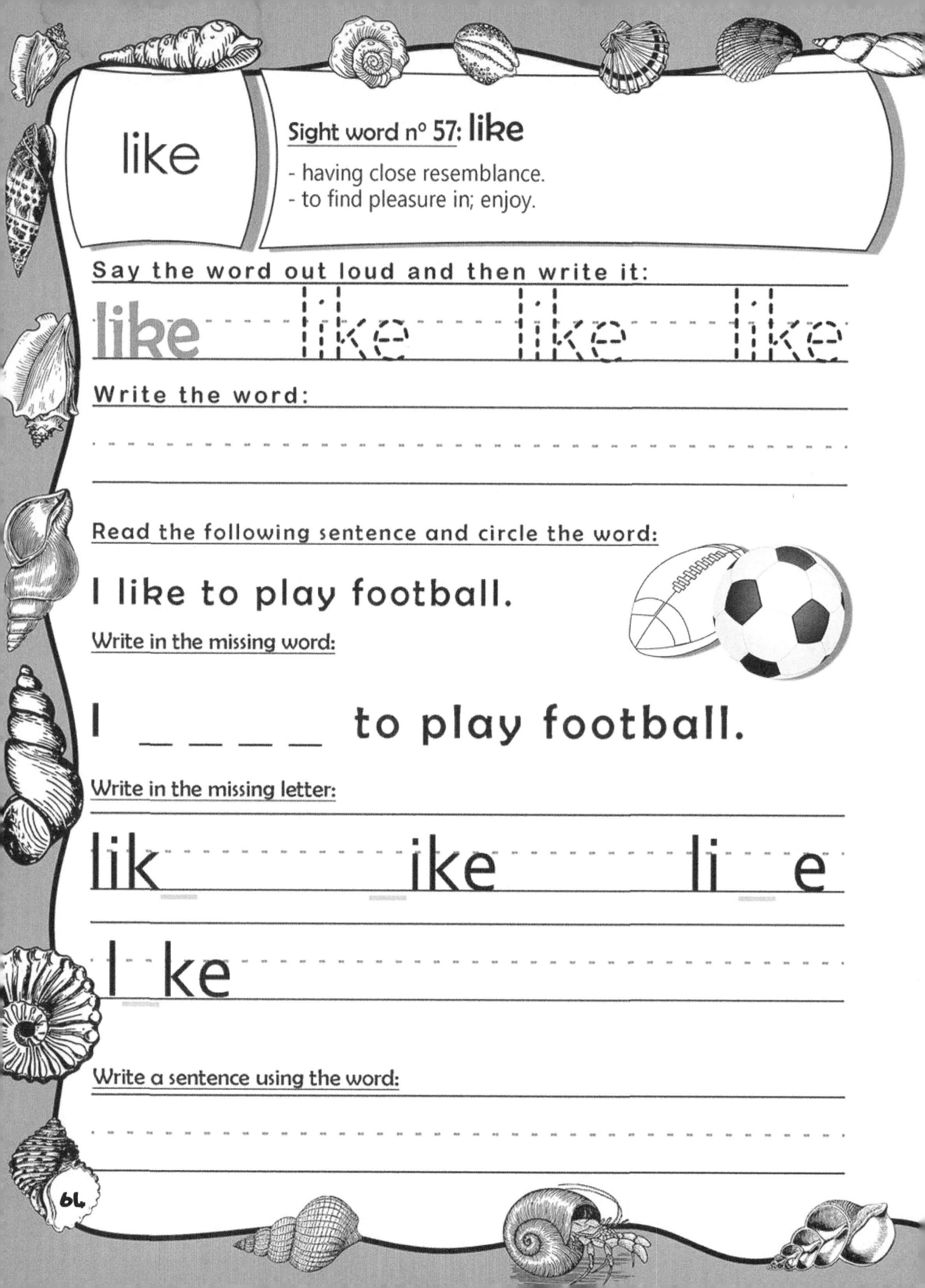

Say the word out loud and then write it:

like   like   like   like

Write the word:

Read the following sentence and circle the word:

I like to play football.

Write in the missing word:

I _ _ _ _ to play football.

Write in the missing letter:

lik＿   ＿ike   li＿e

l＿ke

Write a sentence using the word:

64

Sight word n° 58: **must**
- to be forced to; have to or need to.

must

Say the word out loud and then write it:

must must must must

Write the word:

Read the following sentence and circle the word:

You must attend school.

Write in the missing word:

You _____ attend school.

Write in the missing letter:

mu_t   _ust   mus_

m_st

Write a sentence using the word:

65

new

Sight word n° 59: new
- having recently arrived, been produced, or come into being.

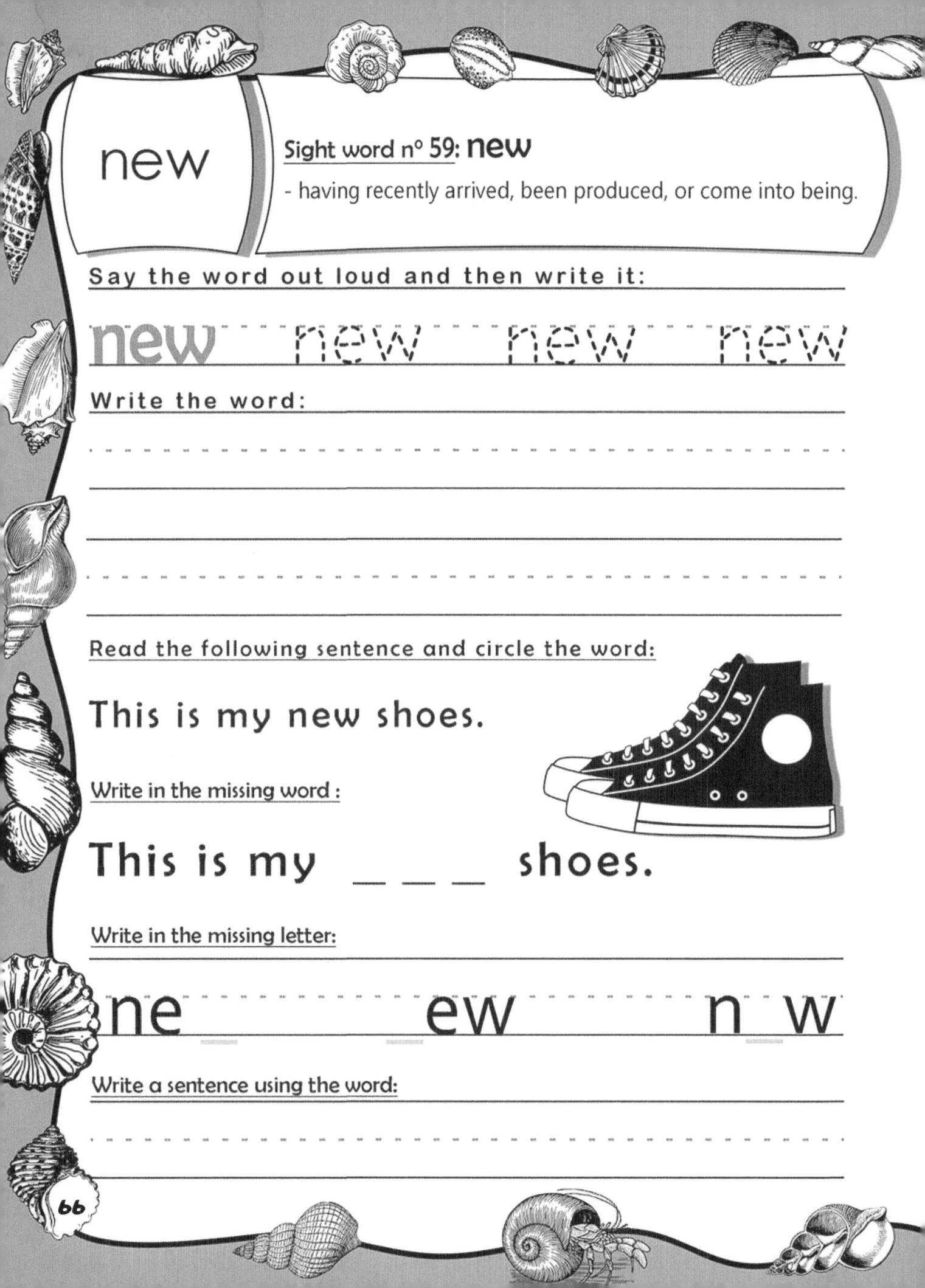

Say the word out loud and then write it:

new   new   new   new

Write the word:

Read the following sentence and circle the word:

This is my new shoes.

Write in the missing word:

This is my ___ shoes.

Write in the missing letter:

 ne   ew   n w

Write a sentence using the word:

Sight word n° 60: **no**
- not so.

no

Say the word out loud and then write it:

no   no   no   no   no

Write the word:

Read the following sentence and circle the word:

no one can beat him.

Write in the missing word:

__ __ one can beat him.

Write in the missing letter:

n   o

Write a sentence using the word:

67

our

Sight word n° 61: our

- belonging to, done by, or having to do with us.

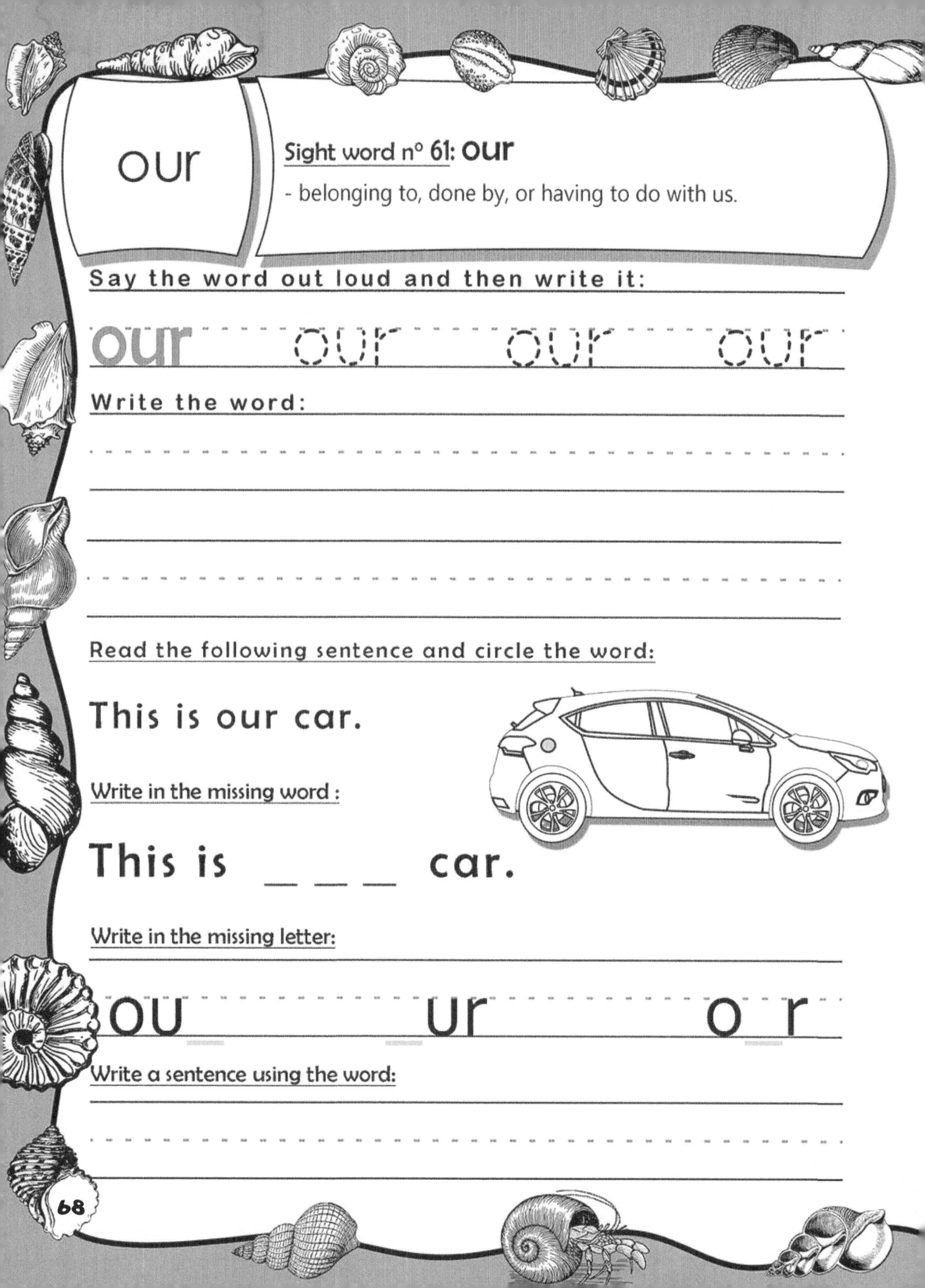

Say the word out loud and then write it:

our   our   our   our

Write the word:

Read the following sentence and circle the word:

This is our car.

Write in the missing word:

This is ___ car.

Write in the missing letter:

ou   ur   o r

Write a sentence using the word:

68

Sight word n° 62: **please**
- to make content or give pleasure to; make happy.
- Kindly.

please

Say the word out loud and then write it:

please   please   please

Write the word:

Read the following sentence and circle the word:

please take a seat over there.

Write in the missing word :

_ _ _ _ _ _ take a seat over there.

Write in the missing letter:

ple_se   p_ease   _lease

plea_e   pleas_   pl_ase

69

out

Sight word n° 63: out
- beyond the limits; away.

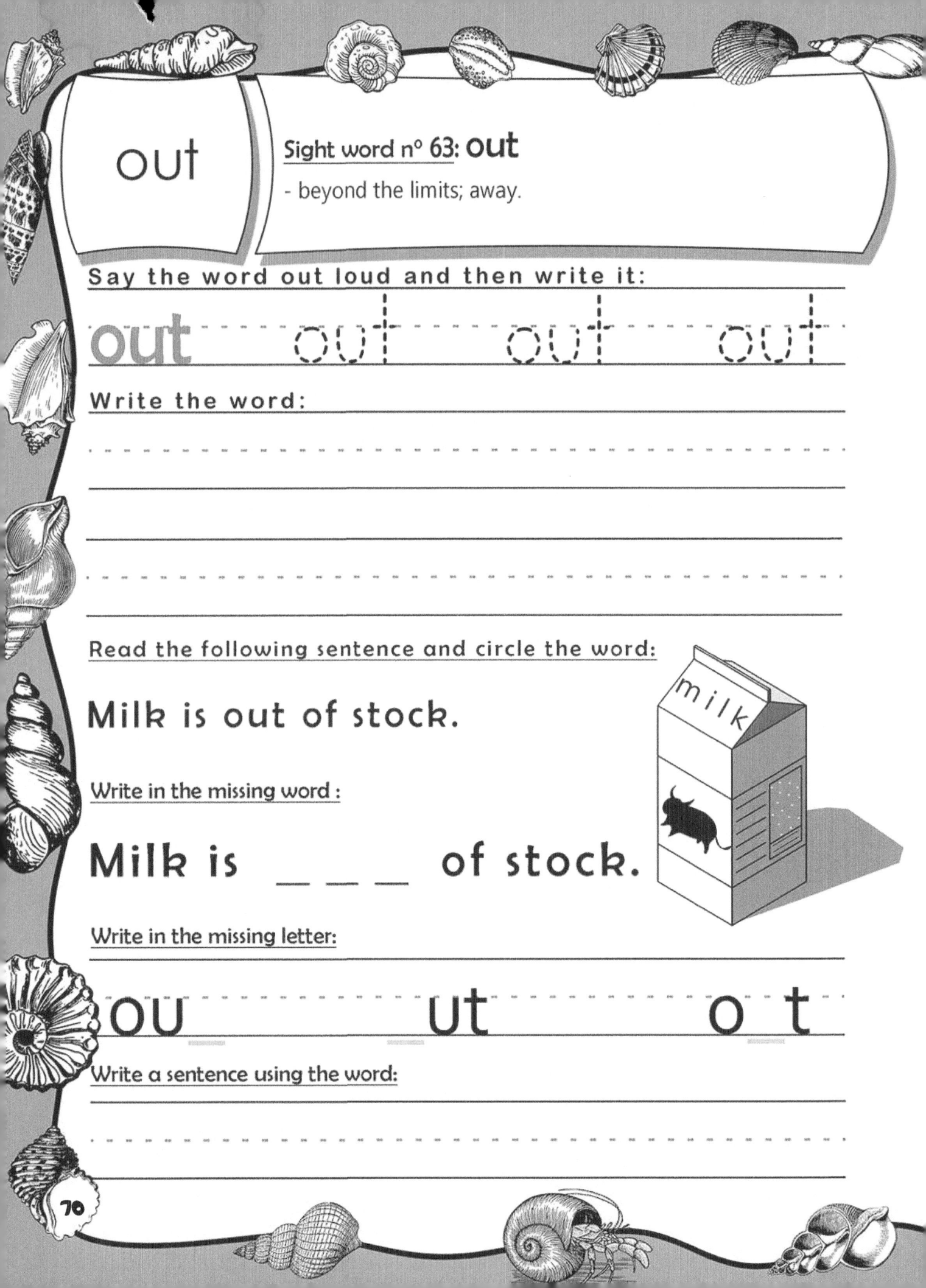

Say the word out loud and then write it:

out   out   out   out

Write the word:

Read the following sentence and circle the word:

Milk is out of stock.

Write in the missing word:

Milk is ___ of stock.

Write in the missing letter:

ou_   _ut   o_t

Write a sentence using the word:

70

Sight word n° 64: **pretty**
- pleasing or attractive to the eyes or ears.

pretty

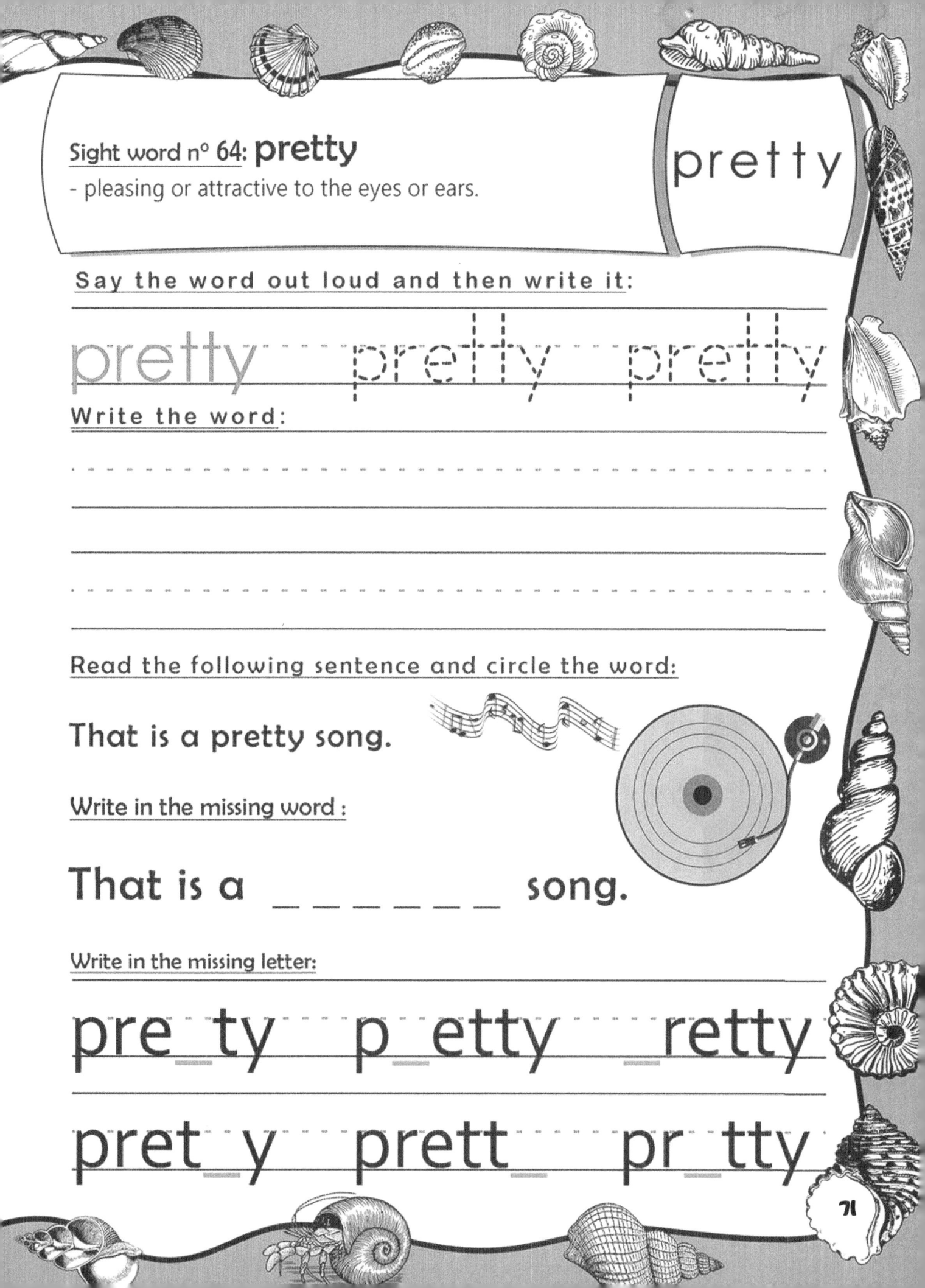

Say the word out loud and then write it:

pretty   pretty   pretty

Write the word:

Read the following sentence and circle the word:

That is a pretty song.

Write in the missing word:

That is a _ _ _ _ _ _ song.

Write in the missing letter:

pre_ty   p_etty   _retty

pret_y   prett_   pr_tty

ran

Sight word n° 65: ran
- to make oneself go forward by moving the legs very quickly (past tense of run).

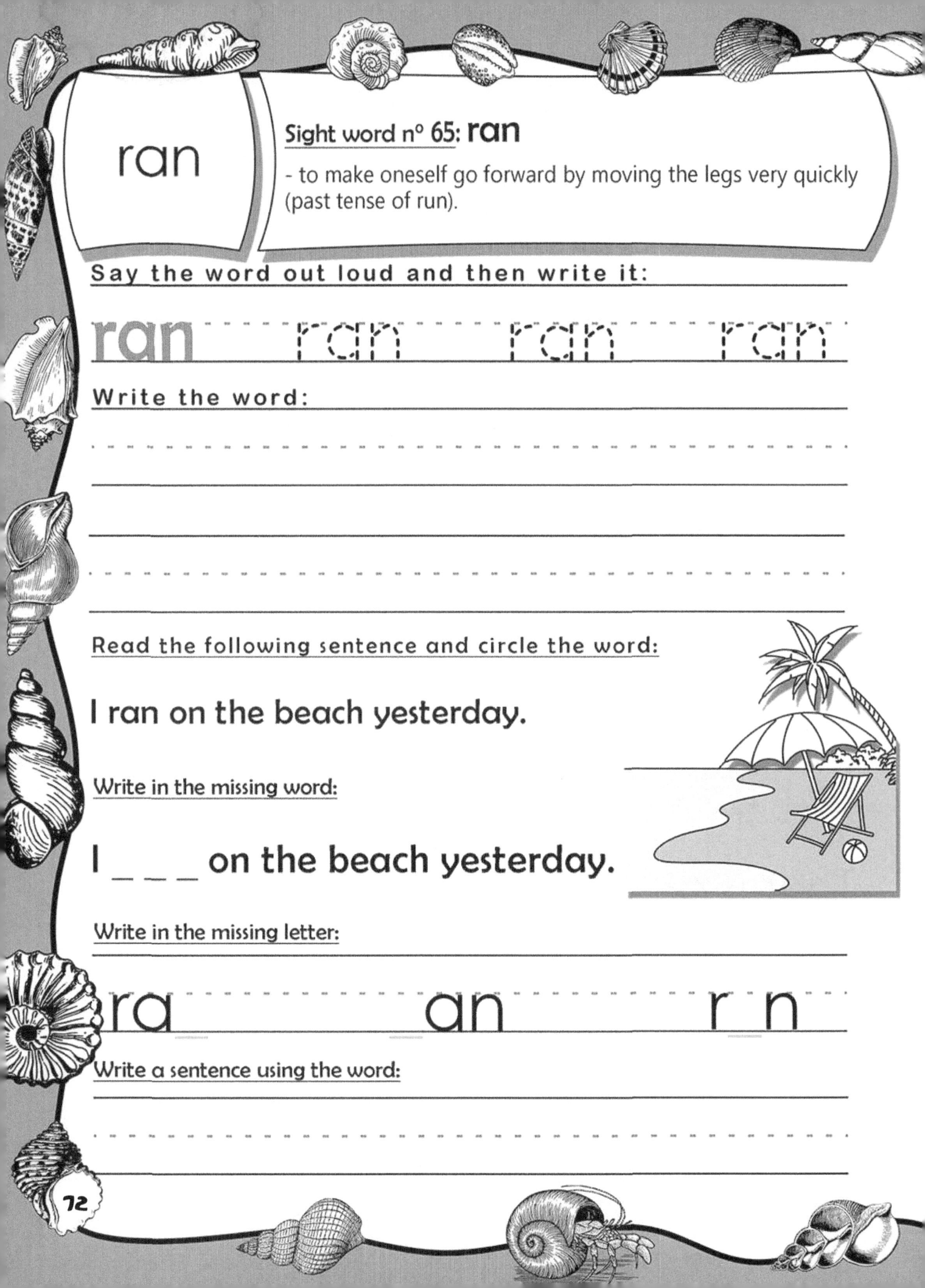

Say the word out loud and then write it:

ran   ran   ran   ran

Write the word:

Read the following sentence and circle the word:

I ran on the beach yesterday.

Write in the missing word:

I ___ on the beach yesterday.

Write in the missing letter:

 ra   an   r n

Write a sentence using the word:

Sight word n° 66: **ride**
- to be carried by a vehicle or animal.

ride

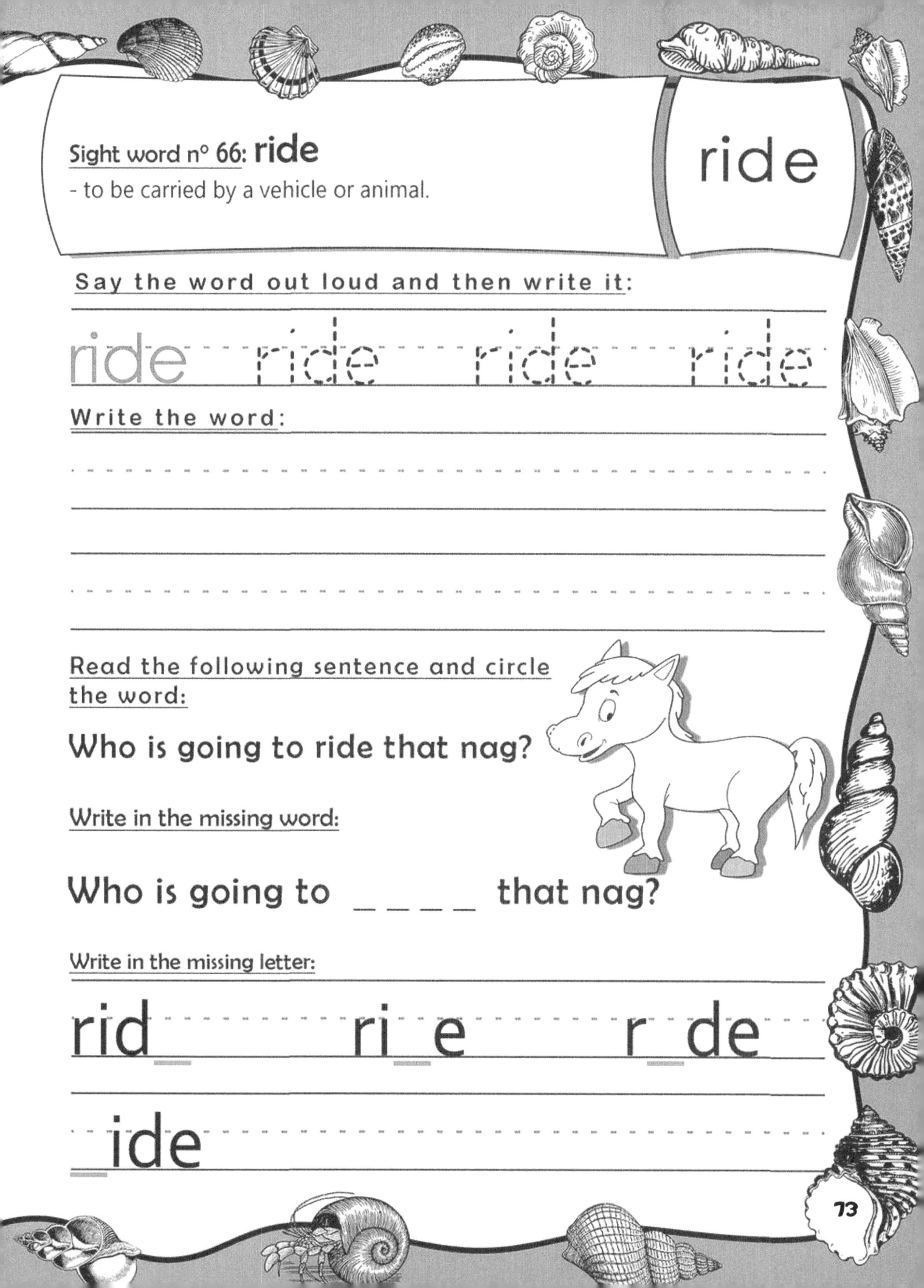

Say the word out loud and then write it:

ride   ride   ride   ride

Write the word:

Read the following sentence and circle the word:

Who is going to ride that nag?

Write in the missing word:

Who is going to ____ that nag?

Write in the missing letter:

rid_   ri_e   r_de

_ide

73

say

Sight word n° 67: say
- to produce (words or sounds) with one's voice.

Say the word out loud and then write it:

say   say   say   say

Write the word:

Read the following sentence and circle the word:

Did you say something?

Write in the missing word:

Did you ___ something?

Write in the missing letter:

sa___   ___ay   s___y

Write a sentence using the word:

Sight word n° 68: SO
- in the way just expressed or indicated.
- to the amount or degree expressed or understood.

so

Say the word out loud and then write it:

so   so   so   so   so

Write the word:

Read the following sentence and circle the word:

I am so happy!

Write in the missing word:

I am _ _ happy!

Write in the missing letter:

s _   _ o

Write a sentence using the word:

she

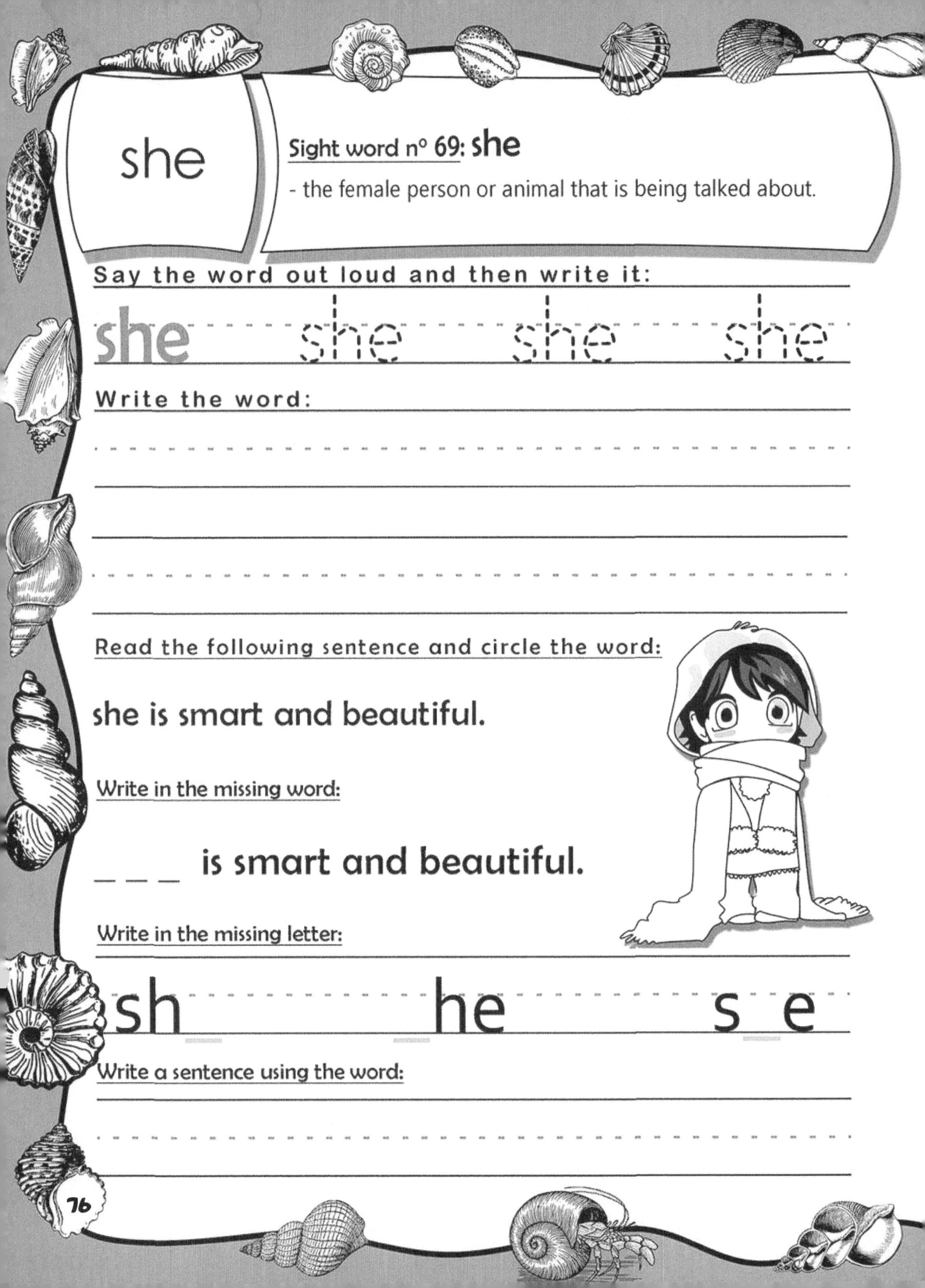

Sight word n° 69: she
- the female person or animal that is being talked about.

Say the word out loud and then write it:

she   she   she   she

Write the word:

Read the following sentence and circle the word:

she is smart and beautiful.

Write in the missing word:

___ is smart and beautiful.

Write in the missing letter:

sh_   _he   s_e

Write a sentence using the word:

Sight word n° 70: **soon**
- in a short time; shortly.

soon

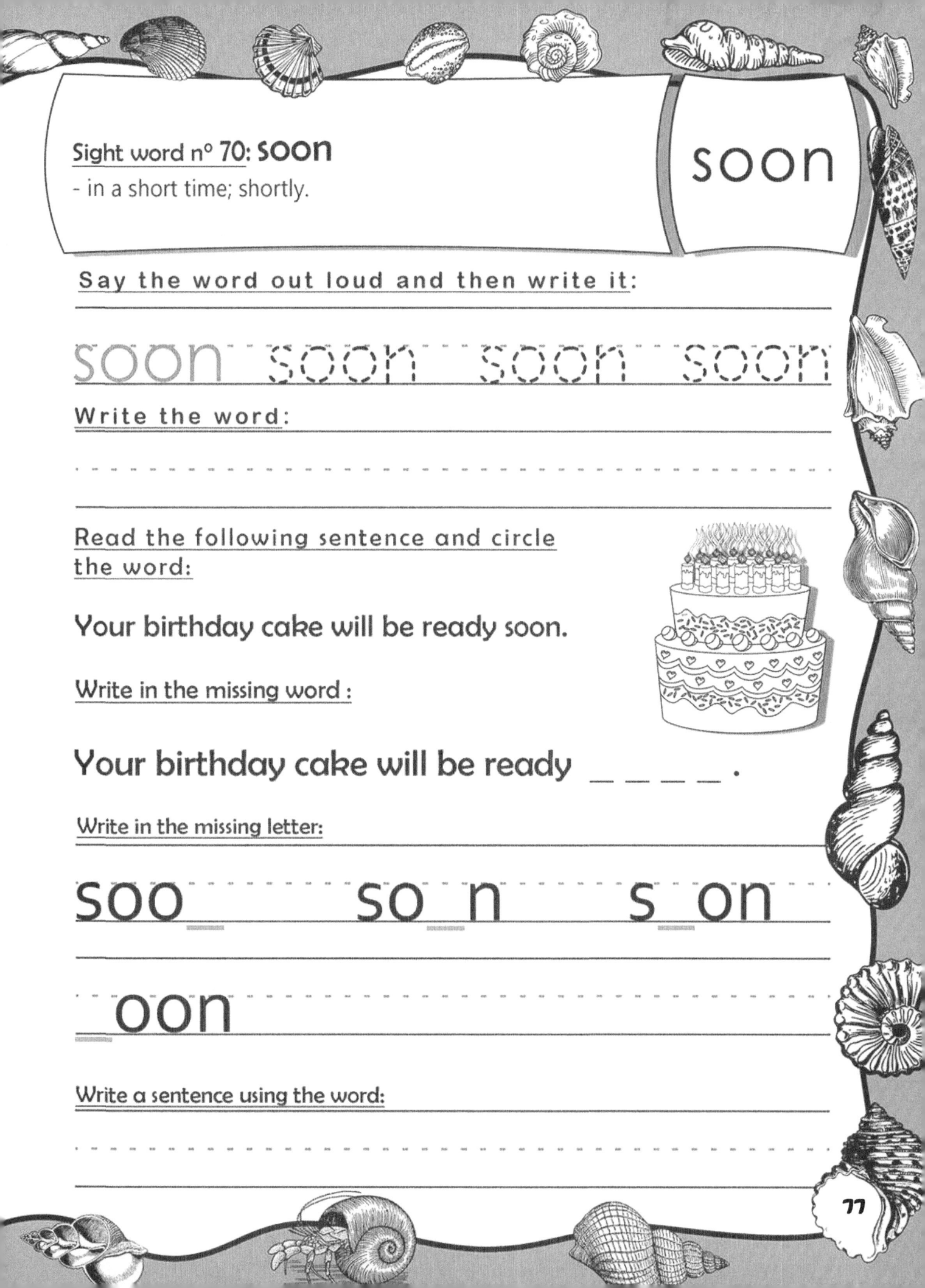

Say the word out loud and then write it:

soon   soon   soon   soon

Write the word:

Read the following sentence and circle the word:

Your birthday cake will be ready soon.

Write in the missing word:

Your birthday cake will be ready ___ ___ ___ ___ .

Write in the missing letter:

soo_   so_n   s_on

_oon

Write a sentence using the word:

that

Sight word n° 71: that

- the person, thing, or matter mentioned or understood.

Say the word out loud and then write it:

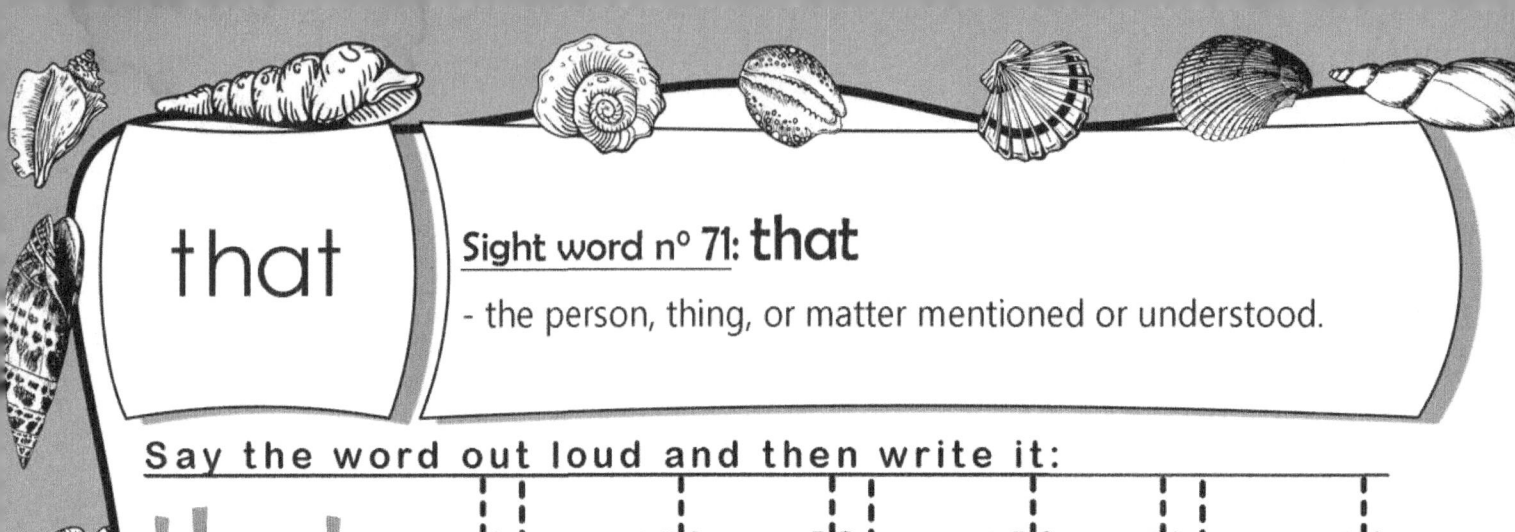

that   that   that   that

Write the word:

_____

_____

Read the following sentence and circle the word:

We train so that we stay healthy.

Write in the missing word in the sentence:

We train so _ _ _ _ we stay healthy.

Find and circle the word:

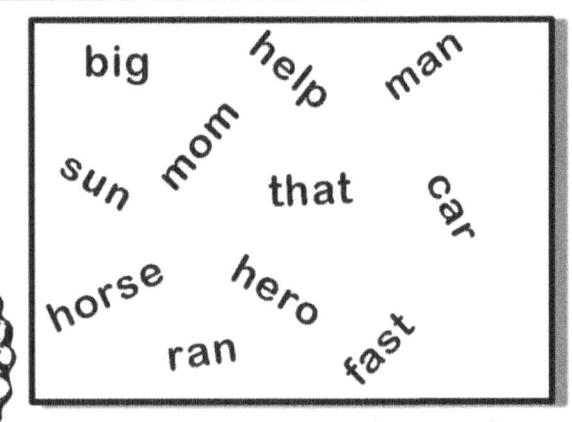

big help man
sun mom that car
horse hero fast
ran

happy store
right cool that
that elephant him
hot cat street

Write a sentence using the word:

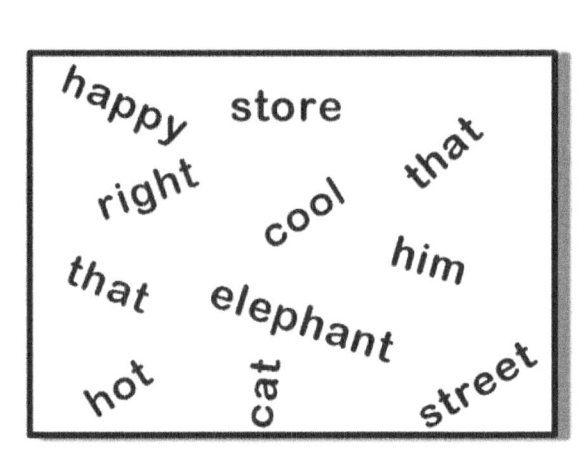

_____

_____

Sight word n° 72: there
- in, at, or to that place.
- at that point.

there

Say the word out loud and then write it:

there   there   there

Write the word:

Read the following sentence and circle the word:

See you there tomorrow evening.

Write in the missing word in the sentence:

Restaurant

See you _ _ _ _ _ tomorrow evening.

Find and circle the word:

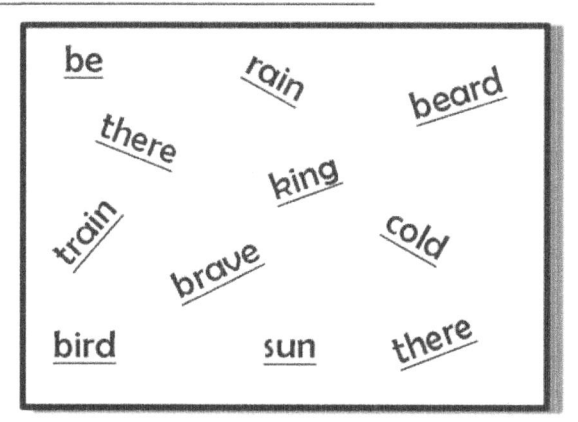

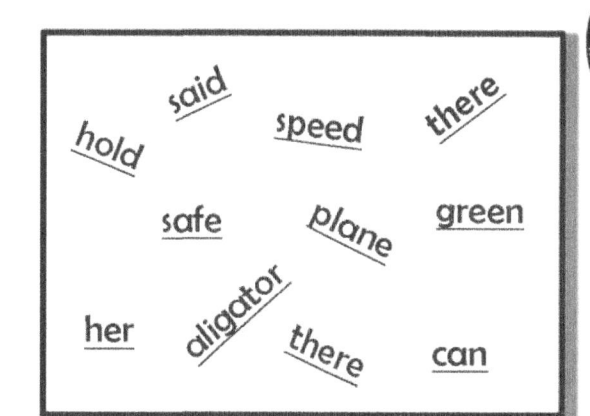

be, rain, beard, there, king, train, cold, brave, bird, sun, there

said, hold, speed, there, safe, plane, green, her, aligator, there, can

Write a sentence using the word:

79

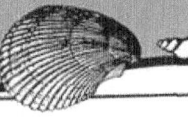

they

Sight word n° 73: they
- the people, things, or animals already being talked about.

Say the word out loud and then write it:

they they they they

Write the word:

Read the following sentence and circle the word:

they say it will be rainy tonight.

Write in the missing word:

_ _ _ _ say it will be rainy tonight.

Find and circle the word:

from   am   by
you   they   for   buy
free   can
they   fast

high   store   dog
they   try
what   them
tree   they
give   sit

Write a sentence using the word:

80

Sight word n° 74: **under**
- below; beneath.

under

Say the word out loud and then write it:

under   under   under

Write the word:

Read the following sentence and circle the word:

The cat is under the table.

Table
cat

Write in the missing word:

The cat is _ _ _ _ _ the table.

Find and circle the word:

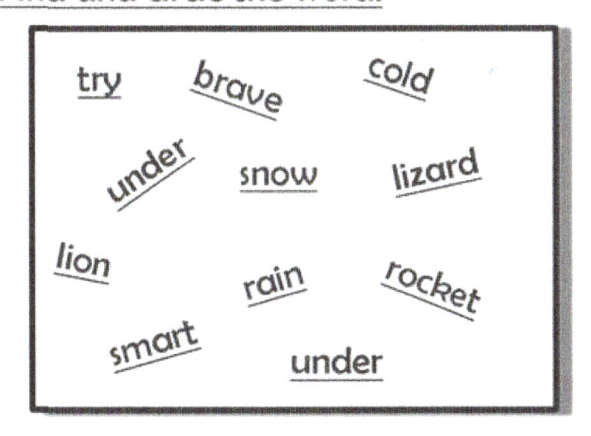

try   brave   cold
under   snow   lizard
lion   rain   rocket
smart   under

long   meal   thin
good   fish   them
down   up   under
they   far   do   high

Write a sentence using the word:

81

this

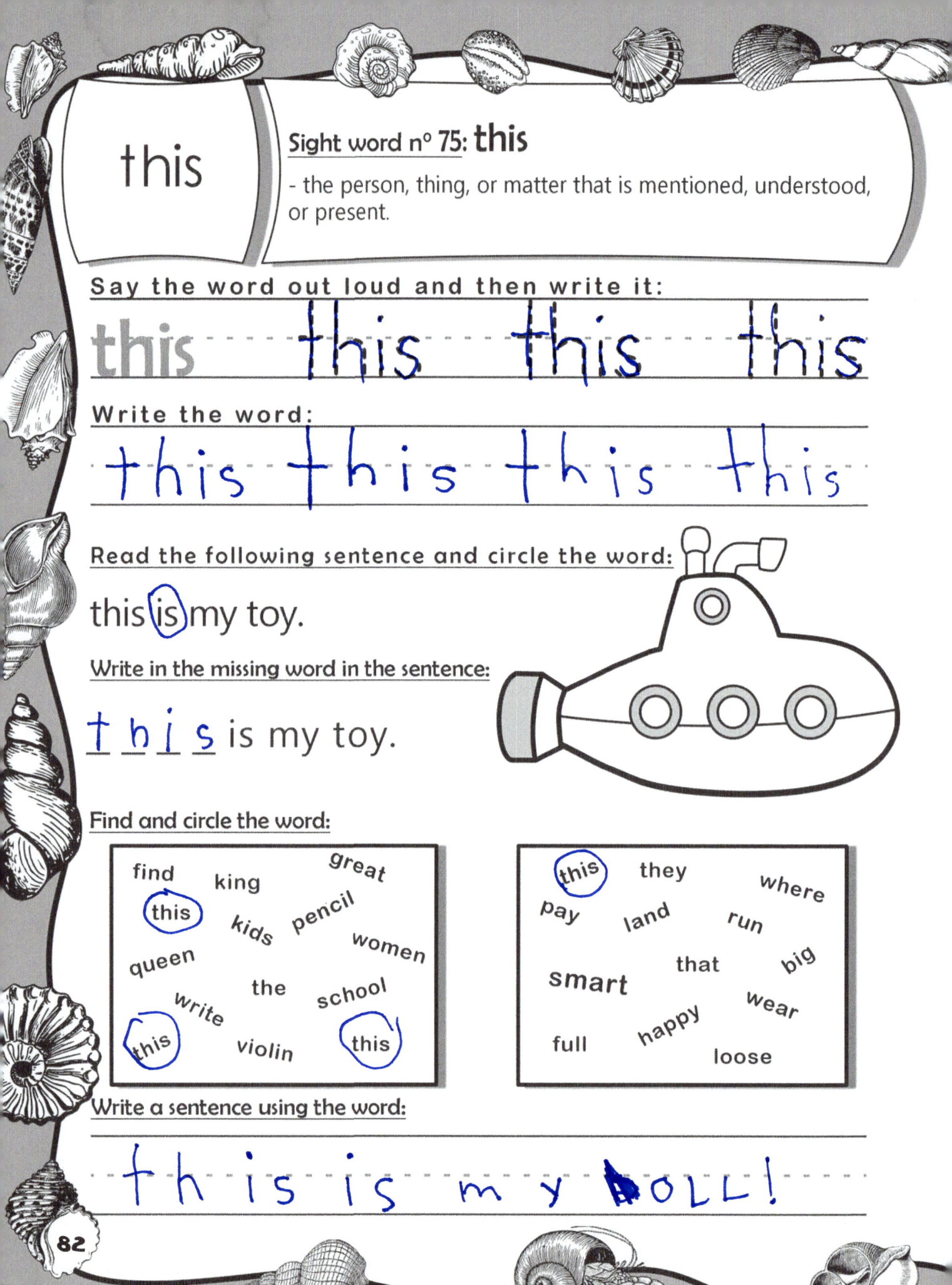

Sight word n° 75: this
- the person, thing, or matter that is mentioned, understood, or present.

Say the word out loud and then write it:

this   this   this   this

Write the word:

this this this this

Read the following sentence and circle the word:

this (is) my toy.

Write in the missing word in the sentence:

t h i s is my toy.

Find and circle the word:

find   king   great
(this)   kids   pencil
queen   women
     write   the   school
(this)   violin   (this)

(this)   they   where
pay   land   run
smart   that   big
full   happy   wear
              loose

Write a sentence using the word:

this is my DOLL!

Sight word n° 76: **want**
- to desire; wish for.

want

Say the word out loud and then write it:

want want want

Write the word:

Read the following sentence and circle the word:

I want to go home.

Write in the missing word:

I _ _ _ _ to go home.

Find and circle the word:

friend have key
pig
bee heavy
hope
dog hand
tiger
start what
want

want snake find
rainbow want
shop
want lake snow
freeze
fire
winner smart want

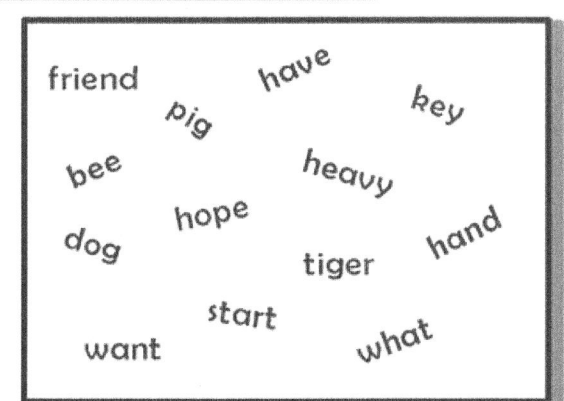

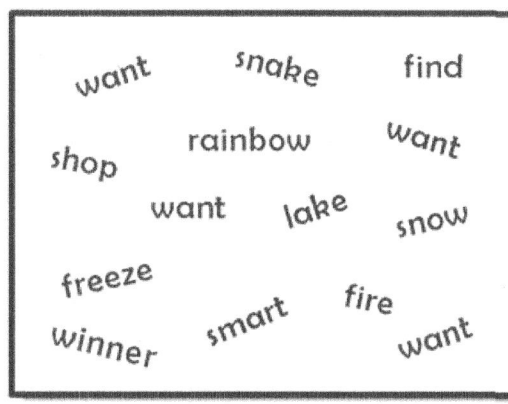

83

too

Sight word nº 77: too
- as well; also; in addition.

Say the word out loud and then write it:

too   too   too   too

Write the word:

_____

Read the following sentence and circle the word:

I want some popcorn too.

Write in the missing word:

I want some popcorn ___ .

Find and circle the word:

fat   they   kuala
giraffe   gum   toy
honey   too   big
tom   limonade
too   too

too   job   lake
fit   terrible   her   say
too   good   too
taste   come
help   too

Write a sentence using the word:

_____
_____

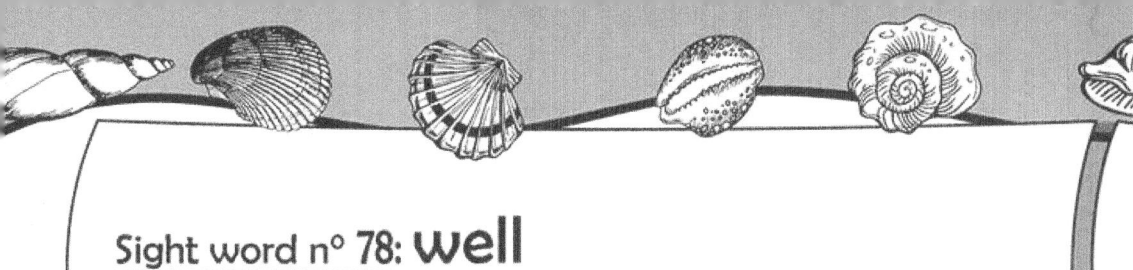

Sight word n° 78: **well**
- in a good, proper, or acceptable way.

well

Say the word out loud and then write it:

well   well   well   well

Write the word:

_____

Read the following sentence and circle the word:

I don't feel very well.

Write in the missing word:

I don't feel very _ _ _ _ .

Find and circle the word:

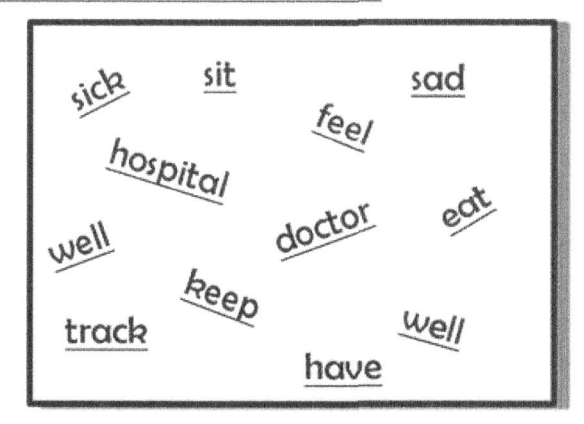

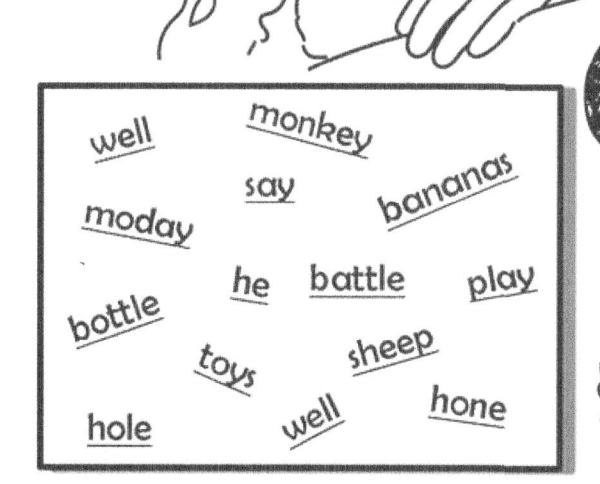

sick   sit   sad
    feel
hospital
         eat
well doctor
   keep   well
 track   have

well   monkey
    say   bananas
moday
    he battle play
bottle
   toys   sheep
hole   well   hone

Write a sentence using the word:

_____

was

Sight word nº 79: was
- a past tense of the verb "be" which means to live or exist.

Say the word out loud and then write it:

was   was   was   was

Write the word:

Read the following sentence and circle the word:

I was sleeping when this happened.

Write in the missing word:

I ___ sleeping when this happened.

Find and circle the word:

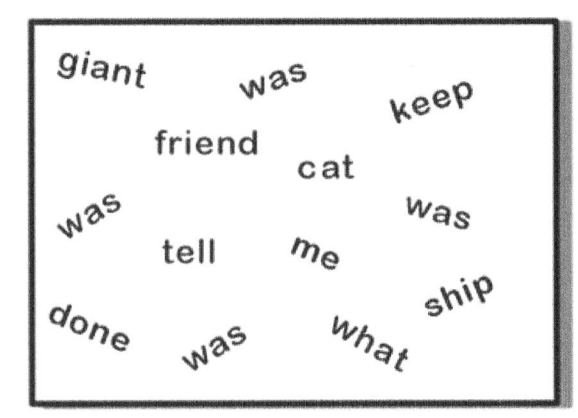

was sing sheet tone work was was his big tongue truck was digger	giant was keep friend cat was was tell me done was what ship

Write a sentence using the word:

Sight word n° 80: **went**
- to move; travel in the past form of verb "go".

went

Say the word out loud and then write it:

went   went   went

Write the word:

- - - - - - - - - - - -

Read the following sentence and circle the word:

Yesterday, I went to visit my grandparents.

Write in the missing word:

Yesterday, I _ _ _ _ to visit my grandparents.

Find and circle the word:

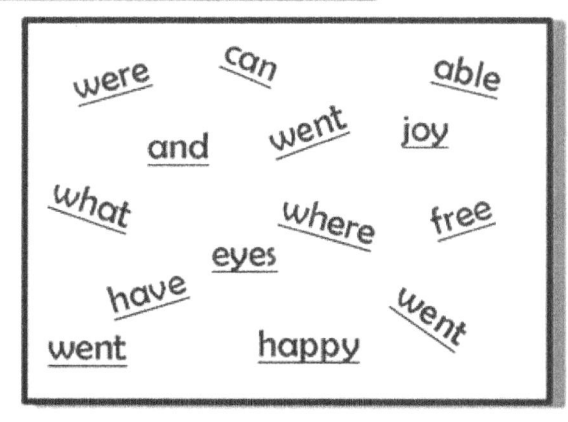

were   can   able
and   went   joy
what   where   free
   eyes
have   went
went   happy

uniform   elephant
   t-shirt   went
went
gun   went   mom
   did   happiness   fat
teacher   went   blank

Write a sentence using the word:

- - - - - - - - - - - -

87

what

Sight word n° 81: what

- which thing or kind of thing.

Say the word out loud and then write it:

what   what   what

Write the word:

_____

Read the following sentence and circle the word:

what are you doing?

Write in the missing word:

_ _ _ _ are you doing?

Find the word and color the apple:

there, big, what, what, did, have

play, what, what, yellow, job, what

Write a sentence using the word:

_____

Sight word n° 82: **white**
- the color of snow or salt; the lightest color.

white

Say the word out loud and then write it:

white   white   white

Write the word:

Read the following sentence and circle the word:

The snowman is white.

Write in the missing word:

The snowman is _ _ _ _ _ .

Find the word and color the pear:

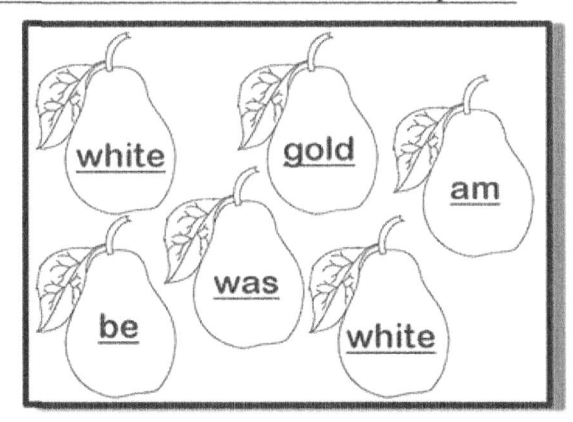

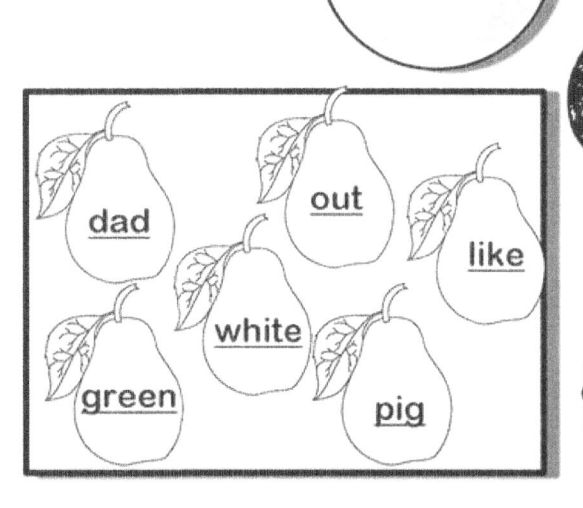

white   gold   am
be   was   white

dad   out   like
green   white   pig

Write a sentence using the word:

89

who

Sight word n° 83: who
- what person or persons.

Say the word out loud and then write it:

who   who   who   who

Write the word:

Read the following sentence and circle the word:

who is on the phone?

Write in the missing word:

_ _ _ is on the phone?

Find the word and color the peach:

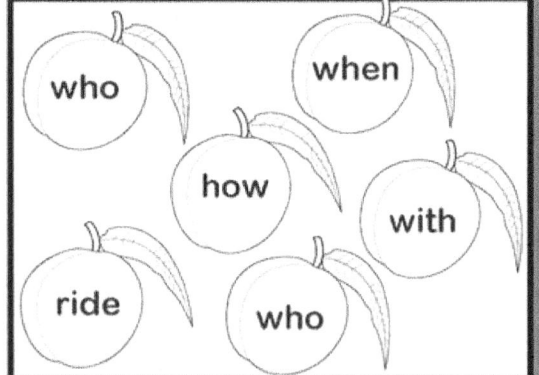

who, when, how, with, ride, who

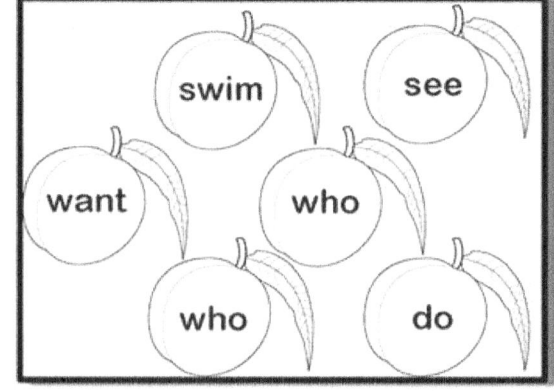

swim, see, want, who, who, do

Write a sentence using the word:

90

Sight word n° 84: **will**
- used to show the future.

will

Say the word out loud and then write it:

will   will   will   will   will

Write the word:

. . . .

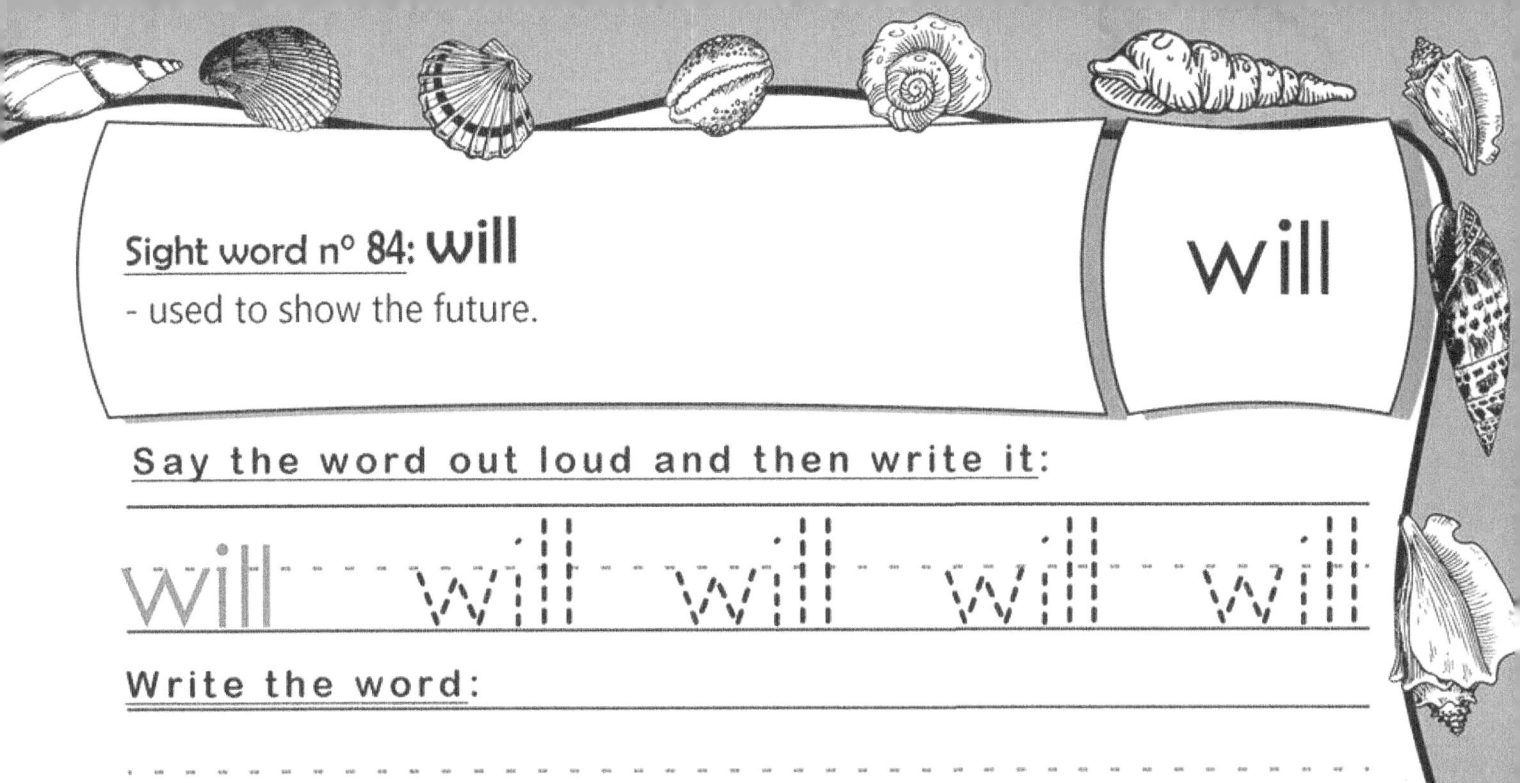

Read the following sentence and circle the word:

Tomorrow will be a holiday.

Write in the missing word:

Tomorrow _ _ _ _ be a holiday.

Find the word and color the pumpkin:

| will | she |
| little | before |

| red | in |
| will | go |

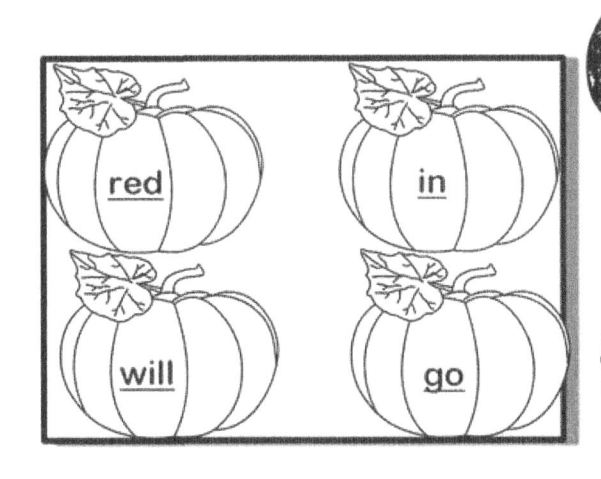

Write a sentence using the word:

. . . .

91

yes

Sight word n° 85: yes

- it is as you say or ask (used to express agreement or acceptance).

Say the word out loud and then write it:

yes   yes   yes   yes

Write the word:

Read the following sentence and circle the word:

Would you like some ice cream? yes, I would.

Write in the missing word:

Would you like some ice cream? _ _ _ , I would.

Find the word and color the orange:

yes   who
         yes
   yes
could   once

door   yes
low   yes
   walk   were

Write a sentence using the word:

92

Sight word n° 86: **with**
- in the company of.

with

Say the word out loud and then write it:

with   with   with   with

Write the word:

Read the following sentence and circle the word:

Eagles are flying with confidence.

Write in the missing word:

Eagles are flying ___ ___ ___ ___ confidence.

Find the word and color the eggplant:

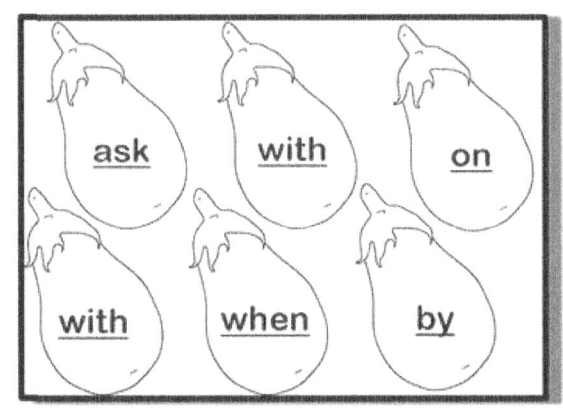

| ask | with | on |
| with | when | by |

| under | without | out |
| left | with | think |

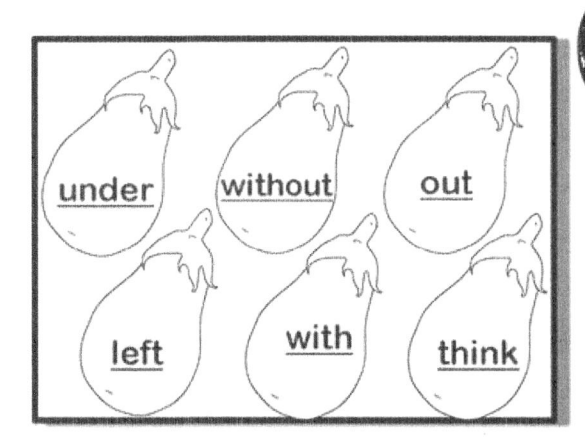

Write a sentence using the word:

93

after

Sight word n° 87: after
- later in time than, or behind in order.
- looking for or in search of.

Say the word out loud and then write it:

after   after   after

Write the word:

Read the following sentence and circle the word:

The cat run after the football.

Write in the missing word:

The cat run _ _ _ _ the football.

Find the word and color the acorn:

| after | behind | allow |
| can | after | up |

| after | truck | green |
| have | with | after |

Write a sentence using the word:

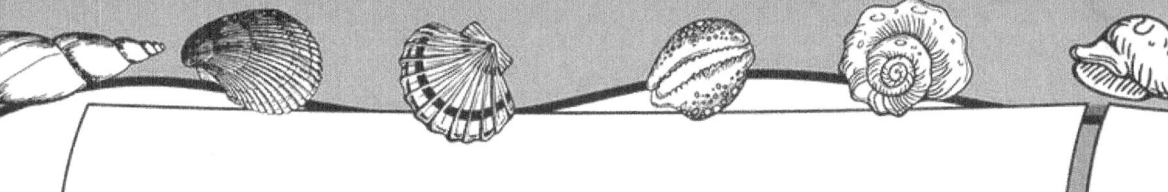

Sight word n° 88: **an**
- another word for a. It is used before words that start with a, e, i, o, or u, or before words that begin with vowel sounds.

an

Say the word out loud and then write it:

an   an   an   an   an

Write the word:

Read the following sentence and circle the word:

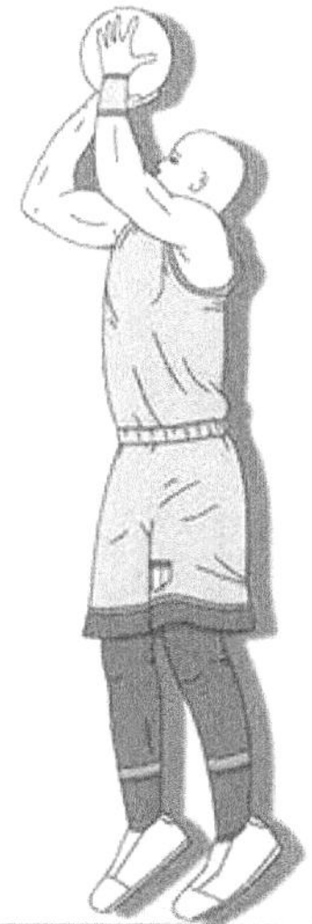

It was an incredible game.

Write in the missing word:

It was __ incredible game.

Find the word and color the bulb:

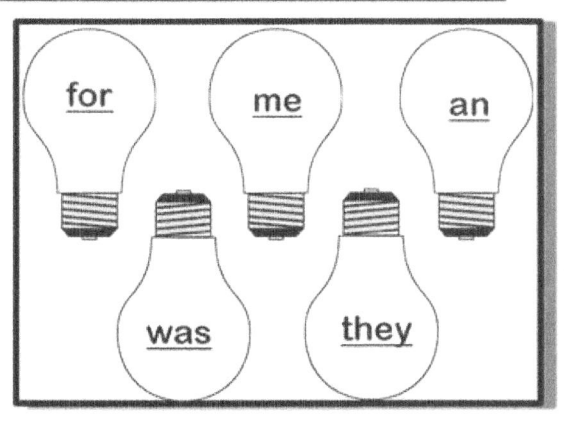

for	me	an
was	they	

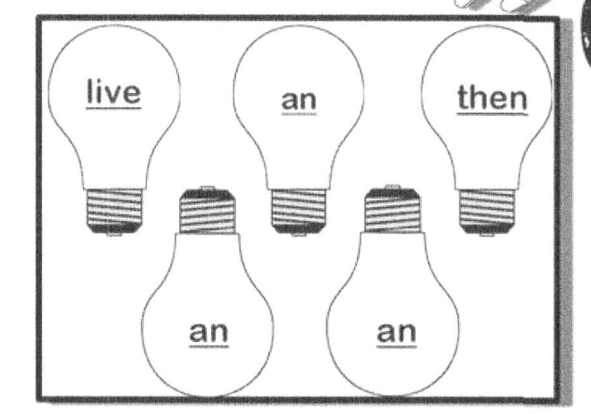

live	an	then
	an	an

Write a sentence using the word:

95

again

Sight word n° 89: again
- one more time; as before.

Say the word out loud and then write it:

again   again   again

Write the word:

_____

Read the following sentence and circle the word:

let's play chess again.

Write in the missing word:

Let's play chess _ _ _ _ .

Find the word and color the tenis ball:

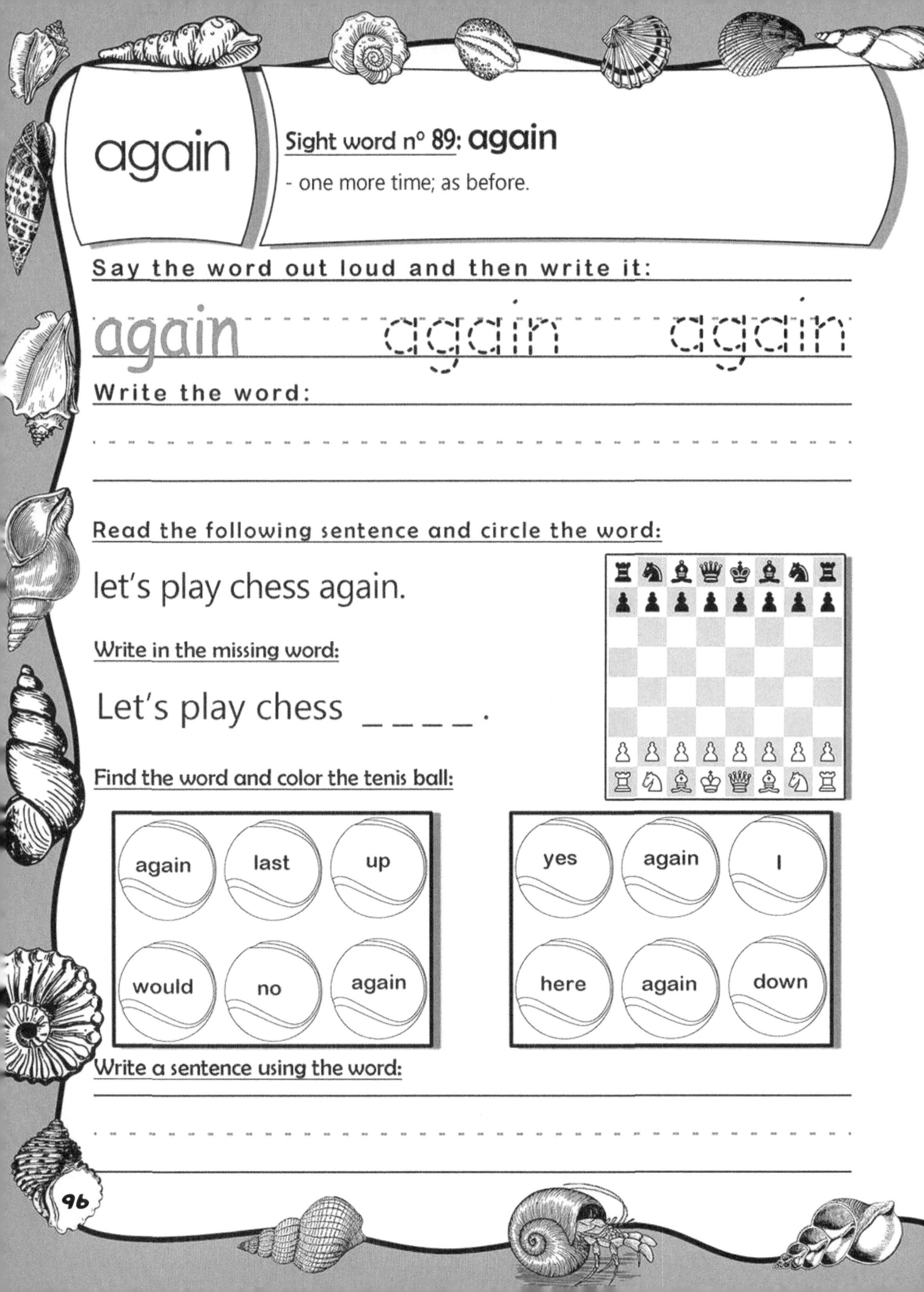

| again | last | up |
| would | no | again |

| yes | again | I |
| here | again | down |

Write a sentence using the word:

_____

Sight word n° 90: **any**
- one or some, no matter which or how many.

any

Say the word out loud and then write it:

any   any   any   any

Write the word:

Read the following sentence and circle the word:

Draw a picture of any animal.

Write in the missing word:

Draw a picture of ___ animal.

Find the word and color the jigsaw:

| any | live | could |
| ask | any | try |

| any | let | may |
| any | over | any |

Write a sentence using the word:

97

as

Sight word n° 91: as

- in equal measure; to the same extent.

Say the word out loud and then write it:

as   as   as   as   as   as

Write the word:

Read the following sentence and circle the word:

He is as strong as his trainer.

Write in the missing word:

He is __ strong __ his trainer.

Find the word and color the tree's part:

Tree 1	Tree 2	Tree 3	Tree 4
put	walk	again	as
try	as	as	down
as	white	thank	buy
want	as	low	as

98

Sight word n° 92: **ask**
- to put a question to.

ask

Say the word out loud and then write it:

ask   ask   ask   ask

Write the word:

Read the following sentence and circle the word:

Can I ask you something?

Write in the missing word:

Can I ___ you something?

Find the word and color the tree:

ask   round   ask   over

Write a sentence using the word:

by

Sight word n° 93: by
- next to; near.
- through the means of; on.

Say the word out loud and then write it:

by   by   by   by   by   by

Write the word:

Read the following sentence and circle the word:

We travel by train.

Write in the missing word:

We travel __ train.

Find the word and color the space:

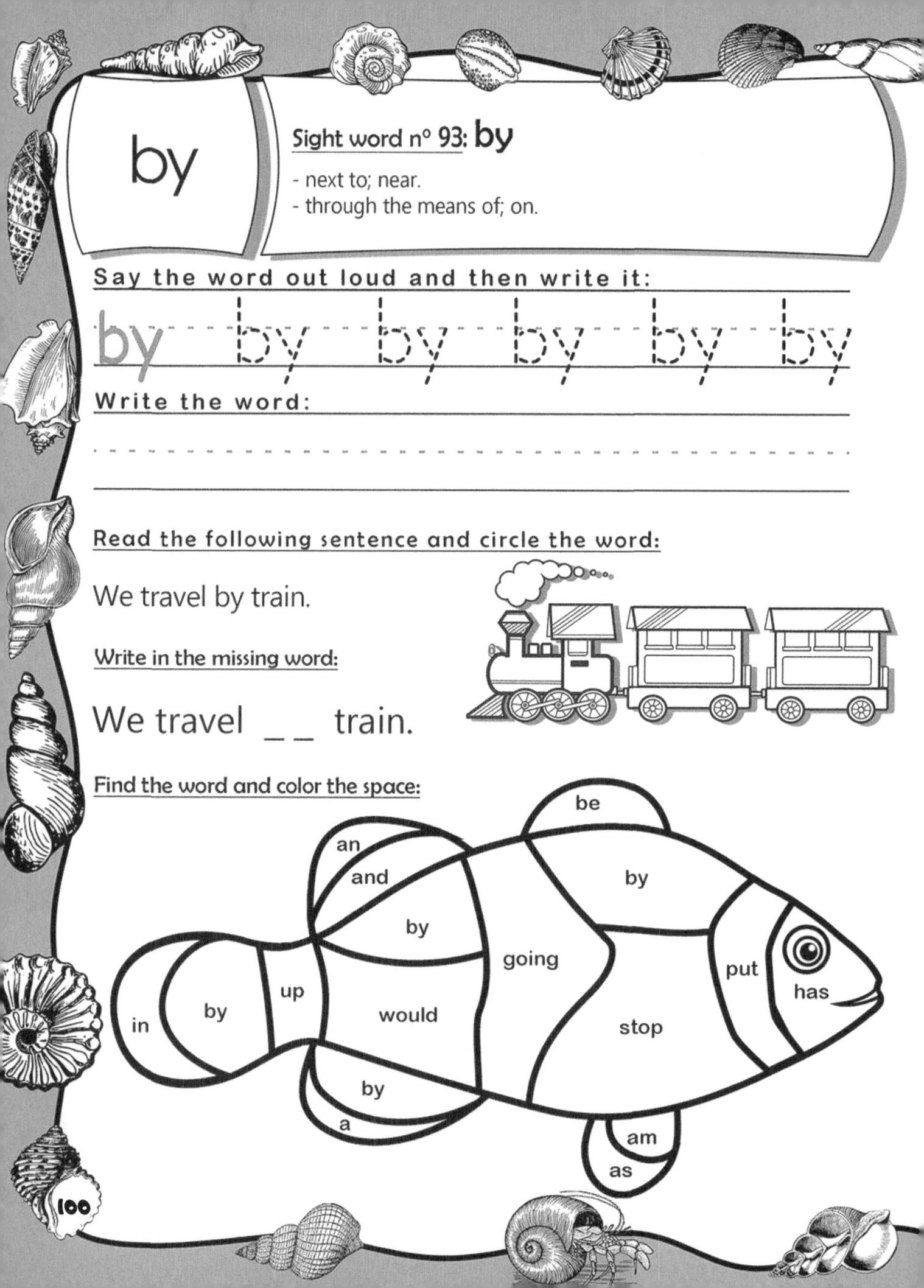

Sight word n° 94: could
- used to express that there was ability to do something in the past, or that an action or state was possible in the past.

could

Say the word out loud and then write it:

could   could   could

Write the word:

Read the following sentence and circle the word:

I wish you could watch that movie.

Write in the missing word:

I wish you _____ watch that movie.

Find the word and color the star:

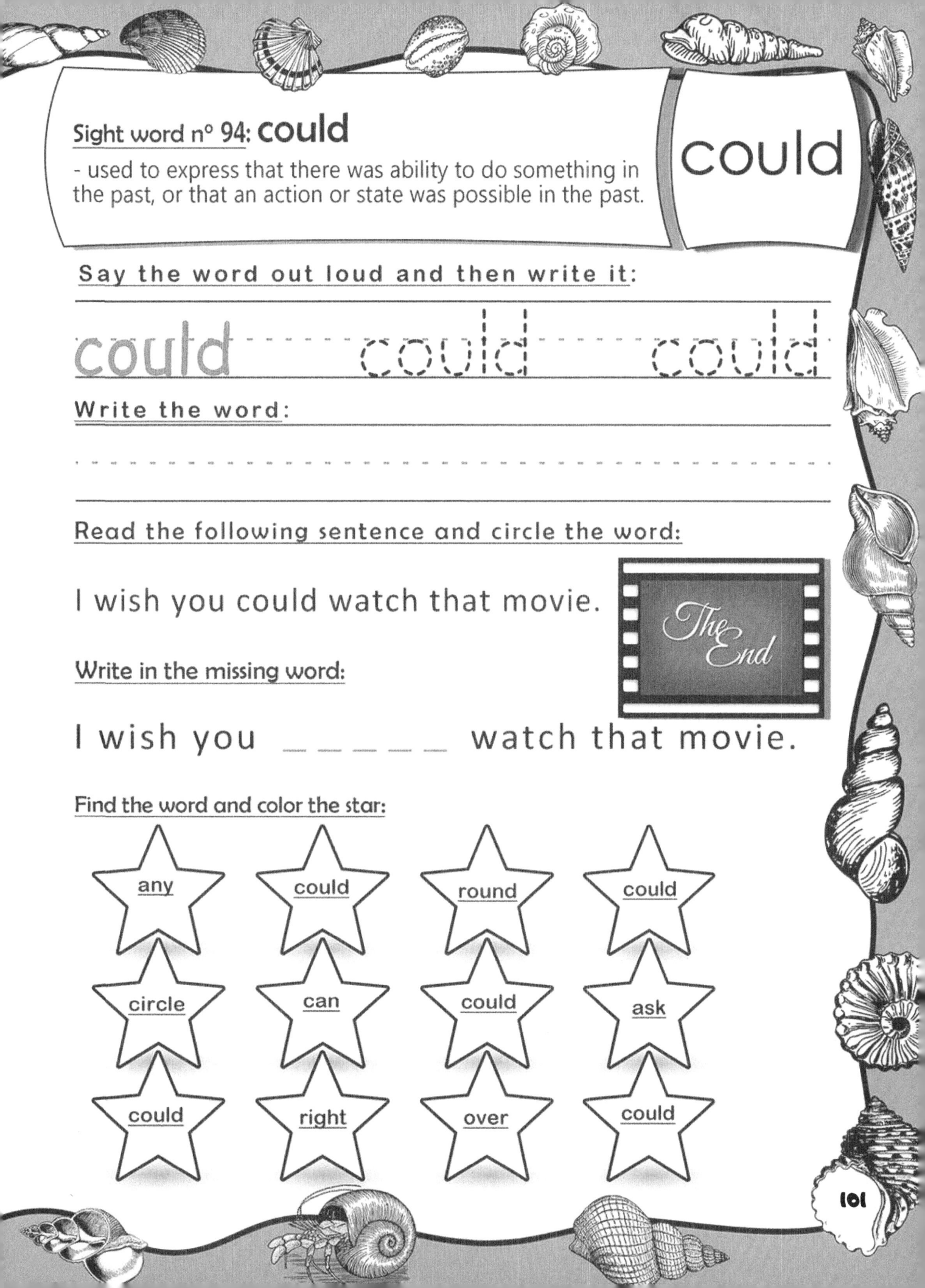

any	could	round	could
circle	can	could	ask
could	right	over	could

fly

Sight word n° 95: fly

- to move through the air by means of wings.
- an insect with two wings.

Say the word out loud and then write it:

fly   fly   fly   fly   fly   fly

Write the word:

....

Read the following sentence and circle the word:

We will fly back home tomorrow.

Write in the missing word:

We will ___ back home tomorrow.

Find the word and color the owl:

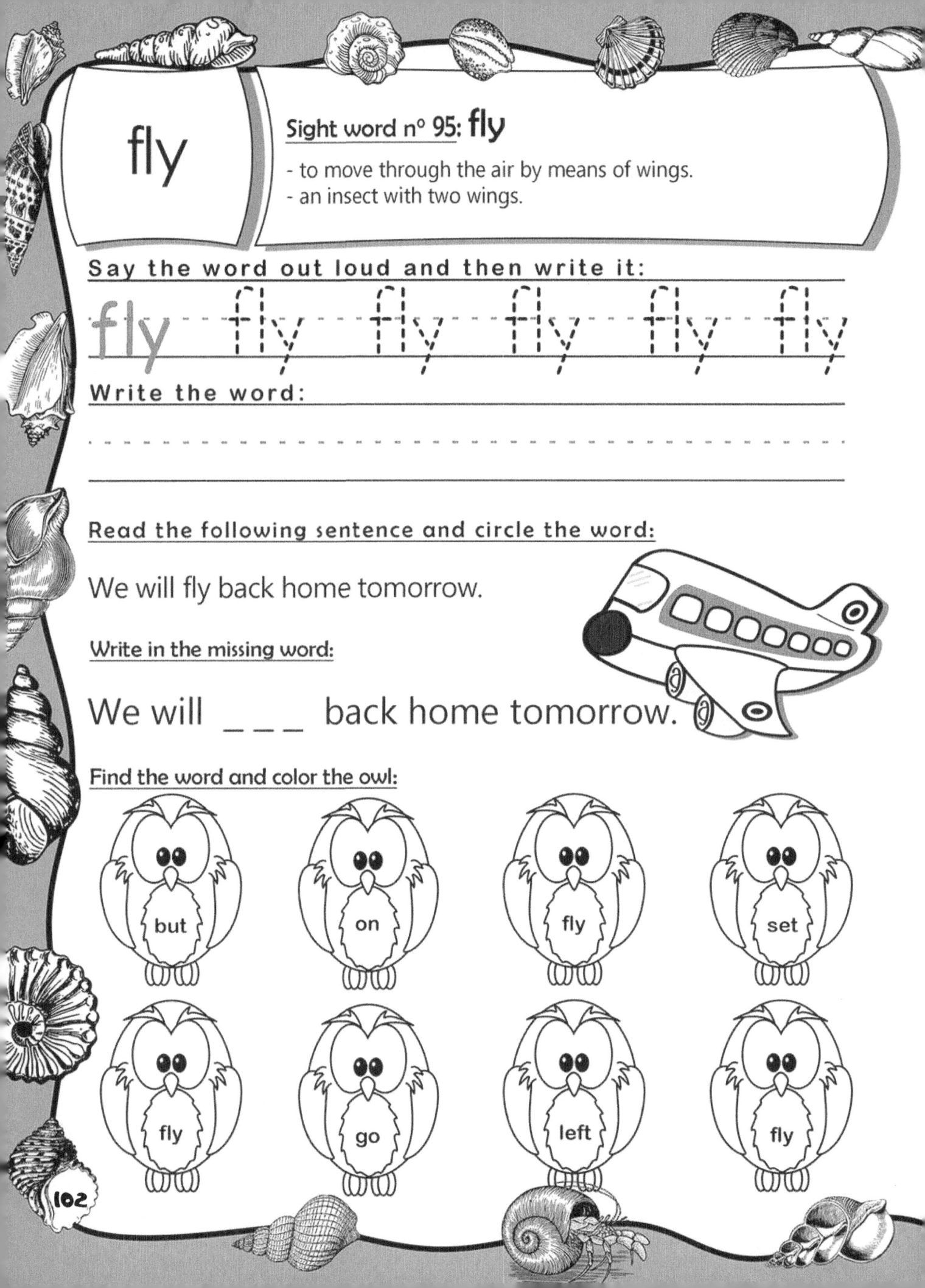

but   on   fly   set

fly   go   left   fly

102

Sight word nº 96: from
- used to show a starting point in place or time.
- used to identify the origin or source.

from

Say the word out loud and then write it:

from   from   from

Write the word:

Read the following sentence and circle the word:

Wood come from trees.

Write in the missing word:

Wood come _ _ _ _ trees.

Find the word and color the part:

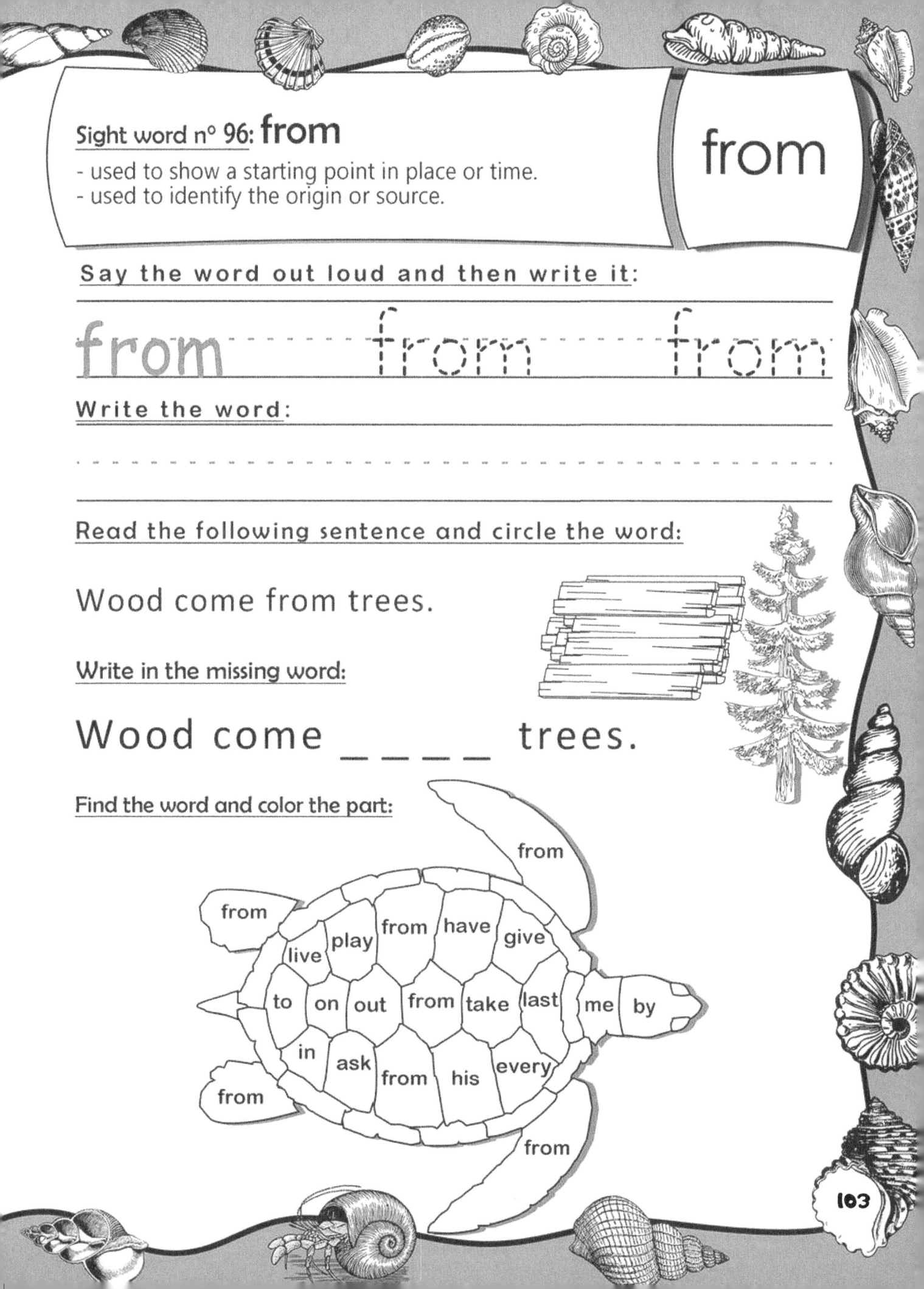

103

going

Sight word nº 97: going
- to move; travel.

Say the word out loud and then write it:

going   going   going

Write the word:

Read the following sentence and circle the word:

I'm going home, it's cold here!

Write in the missing word:

I'm _ _ _ _ _ home, it's cold here!

Find the word and color the space:

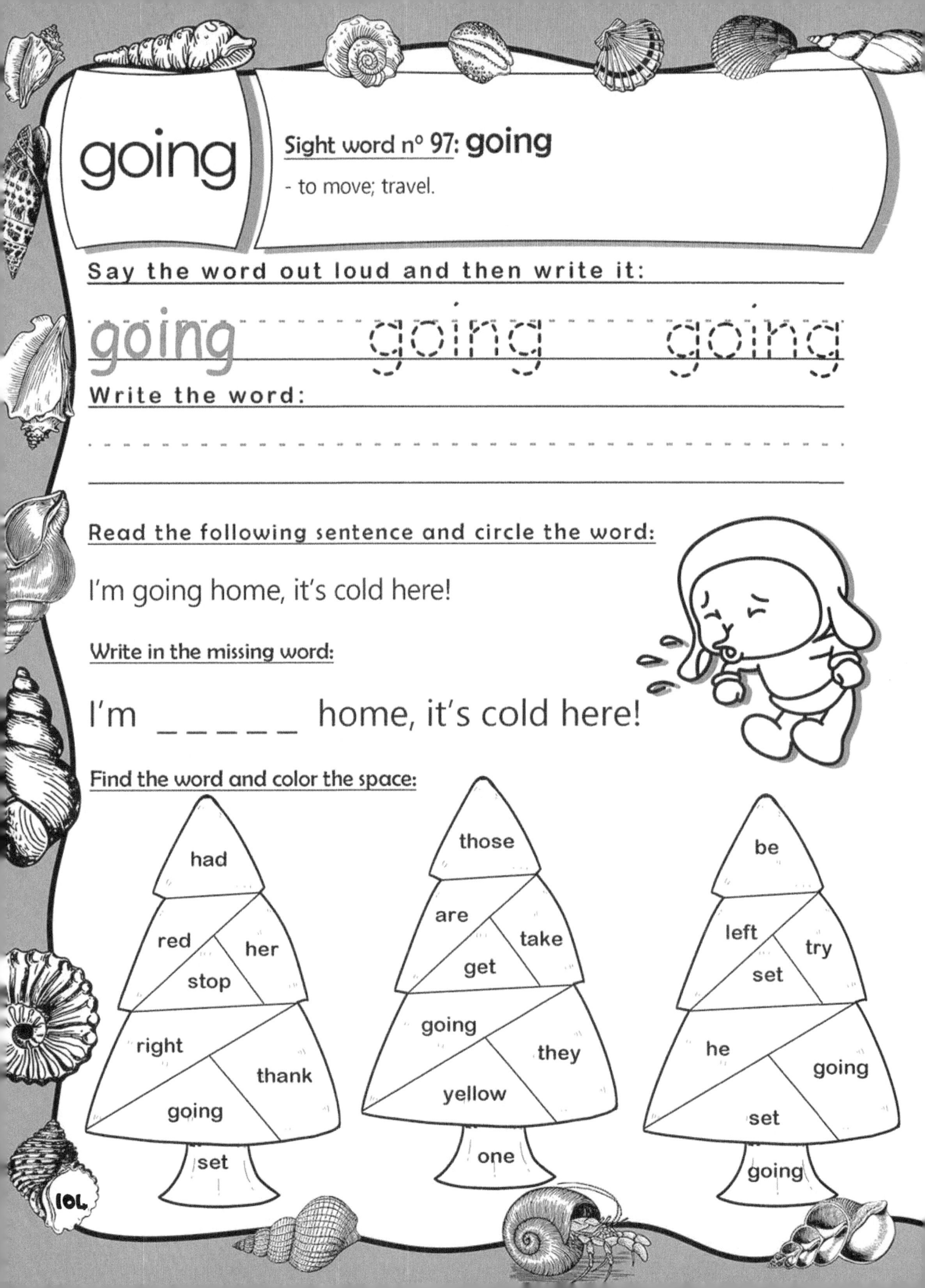

Tree 1: had, red, her, stop, right, thank, going, set

Tree 2: those, are, take, get, going, they, yellow, one

Tree 3: be, left, try, set, he, going, set, going

Sight word n° 98: had
- to own; possess (have in the past).

had

Say the word out loud and then write it:

had   had   had   had

Write the word:

......

Read the following sentence and circle the word:

I had a lot of friends.

Write in the missing word:

I ___ a lot of friends.

Find the word and color triangle:

had	his	had	little
pay	could	pay	had
would	had	think	walk
had	open	then	had

105

has

Sight word n° 99: has

- to own; possess.

Say the word out loud and then write it:

has   has   has   has

Write the word:

Read the following sentence and circle the word:

He has a pet dog.

Write in the missing word:

He ___ a pet dog.

Find the word and color the petal:

Sight word n° 100: **how**
- by what manner or means.
- in what way, state, or condition.

how

Say the word out loud and then write it:

how   how   how   how

Write the word:

Read the following sentence and circle the word:

I don't know how to play piano.

Write in the missing word:

I don't know ___ to play piano.

Find the word and color cactus:

a — to / how / love / be — just / has

on — how / what / live / in — let / how

am — him / out / take / thank — how / please

SHORT U

Write the first letter of each picture's name to spell the **short u** words.

~~bug~~ ~~gum~~ ~~hug~~ ~~cup~~ ~~fun~~ ~~mud~~ sun ~~pup~~

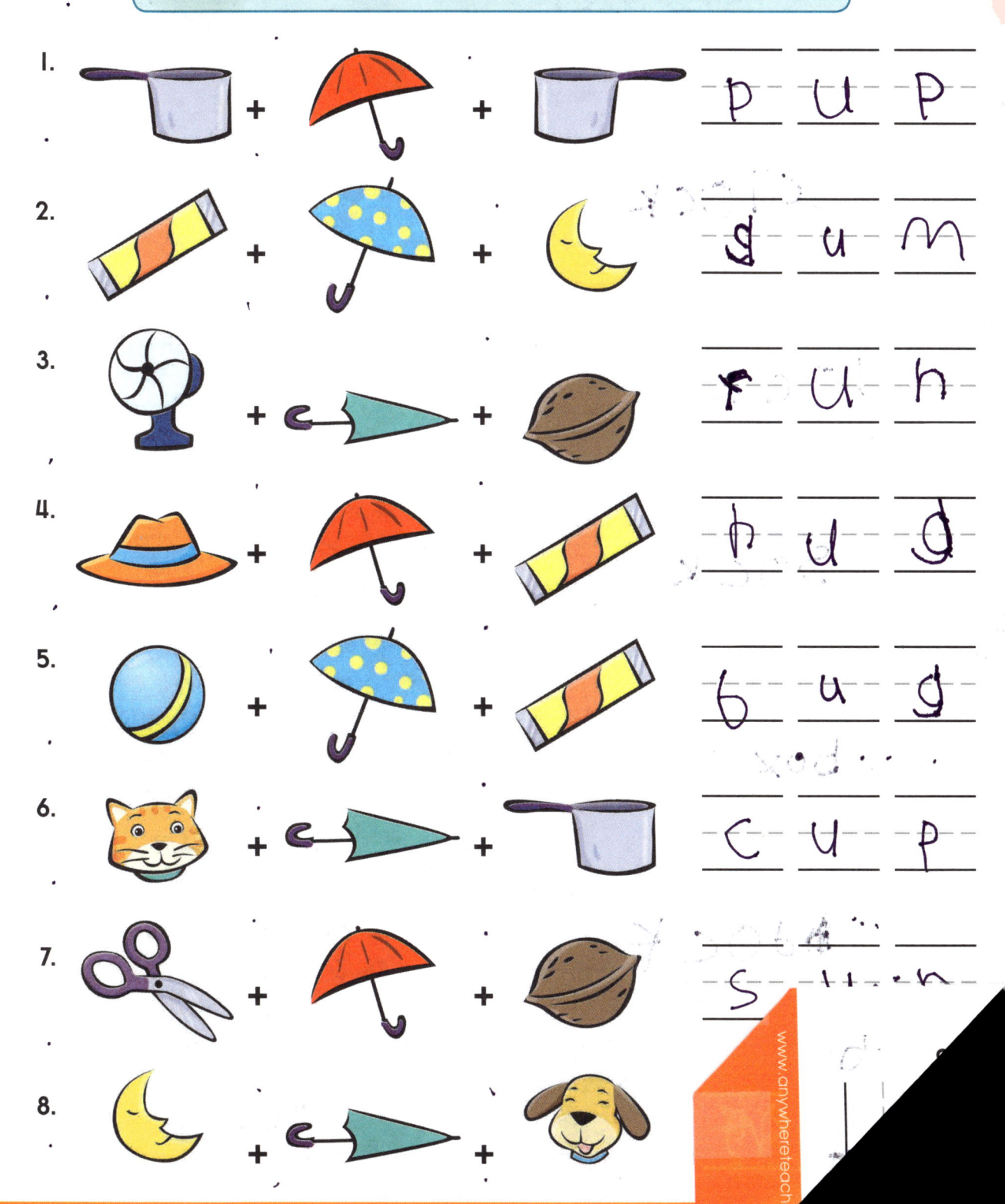

1. pot + umbrella + pot = p u p
2. gum + umbrella + moon = g u m
3. fan + umbrella + nut = f u n
4. hat + umbrella + gum = h u g
5. ball + umbrella + gum = b u g
6. cat + umbrella + pot = c u p
7. scissors + umbrella + nut = s u n
8. moon + umbrella + dog =

SHORT O

Write the **short o** words to answer the riddles.

rock box sock dock lock clock

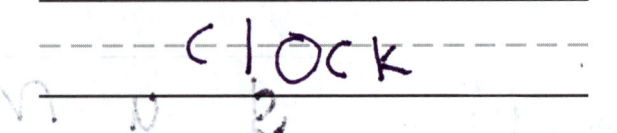

1. It tells you the time.
   clock

2. A key opens it.
   lock

3. You wear it on your foot.
   sock

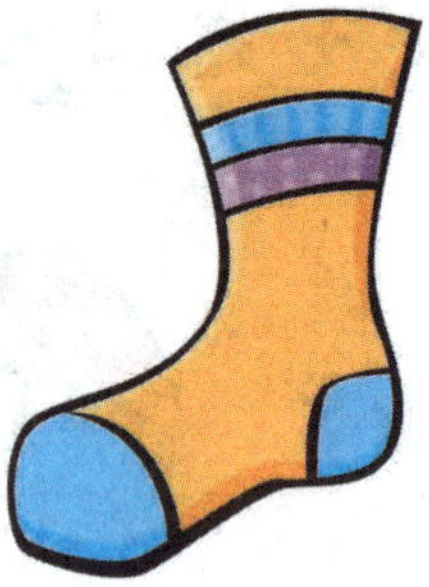

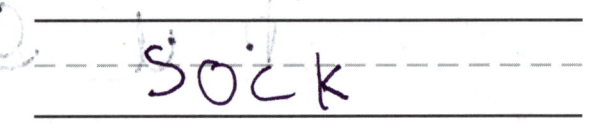

4. You put things in it.
   box

5. A boat can be here.
   dock

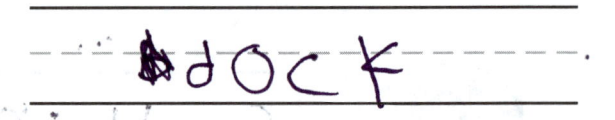

6. It is hard.
   rock

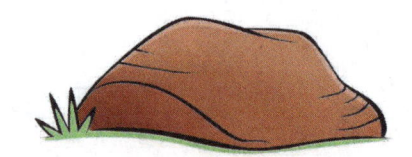

Author's letter:

Hello dear reader,

I created this "Sight Words" book to help toddlers, pre-k and preschoolers to learn to write and read these important words. I tried to add some reliable pictures in every page to help them recognize the word fast, and to attract their attention to the book. I also added a variety of activities to help them memorize the words easily.

Hope this helped your kid(s) well, if not so much or if you have any issues with this book please don't hesitate to write a honest review at the book page on Amazon. I will be very happy to read your feedbacks.

Also if you like the book let us know that in a few lines review.

Stay safe and be happy!

Cheers!

S&M Readers

Christmas gift:

Christmas is coming! So I made 10 gift cards worth of $10 each for you,

To participate in the poll to win one of these gift cards (you can get an extra gift for your kids for the Christmas holidays), just send "my SW gift card" to this email: atomipublishing90@gmail.com

We will be sending gifts to the winners starting from October 31st 2020. Good luck everyone!

Made in the USA
Middletown, DE
02 October 2020